Marilyn ,

With Love ♡

Taylor

Rox

Awakening

A Journey to Uplift and to Enlighten

TAYLOR ROSE

BALBOA.
PRESS

A DIVISION OF HAY HOUSE

Balboa Press books may be ordered through booksellers or by contacting:

Balboa Press
A Division of Hay House
1663 Liberty Drive
Bloomington, IN 47403
www.balboapress.com
1 (877) 407-4847

Print information available on the last page.

ISBN: 978-1-5043-5062-4 (sc)
ISBN: 978-1-5043-5064-8 (hc)
ISBN: 978-1-5043-5063-1 (e)

Library of Congress Control Number: 2016903057

Balboa Press rev. date: 3/10/2016

∞CONTENTS∞

Awake

I rise, I see
All that is meant to be,
Surrounds, confounds,
Until we
All rise, awaken, and see that
We are
One.

∞PROLOGUE∞

Imagine what it would feel like, what it would be like, if you could inhabit a space that would allow you to live a life on earth that is richer, deeper, and fuller than anything you could ever conceive. Does this space even exist? If it does, can we access it? The answer to both is yes. This space exists. We <u>can</u> access it. The space is a realm without bounds, a space where knowledge, wisdom, and answers lie. When we are able to access this space, we may use these tools to enrich our lives on earth; to receive the most life has to offer, to fulfill our destinies, and to achieve enlightenment. The key to unlocking it all is awakening. We must awaken to the existence of this space, to the power we possess within ourselves, and to the thought that we are meant to see more in life than our physical realities and circumstances so that we may grow, learn, and blossom into the beings we have the full potential of being. It is in this space of light that we become aware of life's purpose and the lessons to be learned so that our human experience is everything and more that it can be. The space is not separate from us or difficult to reach; it is within us and around us, and all we must do is make the conscious decision to be open to connecting with this space and invite it into our lives. In doing so, our journey of awakening begins. This journey is inspiring, arduous, illuminating, and necessary for each soul to undertake, and from one soul to another, the journey is not something to be missed. The steps along the way, and the resulting experiences are nothing short of extraordinary. This book promises to open your eyes to a whole new world, to uplift, and to inspire you on this journey of life. Let us all awaken.

∞TRIGGERS∞

Guided Trigger

We each have a trigger that signals
us to make a change,

To follow a new direction, that will transform
our lives and our spirits in more than one way.

At first, solitude calls our name, washing
away that which cannot stay.

Then comes the climb to new heights, at
times arduous, leaving you dazed.

But then, the floodgates burst open,
and you will see the light of day.

A new being will emerge, stronger
and wiser than before.

It never ends, it only bends, as you
are guided to turn once more.

∞TRIGGERS∞

We all have a light within us; a spark of Divinity. The potential to awaken and live an enlightened life. We are born with this potential, and when the time is right, we begin the process of awakening into a more enlightened being. Why must we all awaken and undertake a spiritual journey? Whether conscious or not, we are all seeking answers to life's questions, the truth, purpose, greater connection, or meaning. Awakening provides answers and allows us to find what we are searching for. In awakening, we become more wise, more enlightened and fulfilled, a completeness that may only be experienced through awakening; no other earthly experience compares to it. This is our spiritual journey. It is deeply personal; we each have our own, and the process is different for us all. Some details are the same for every journey, we all have lessons to learn, strides to make, and missions to fulfill. The actual experiences and lessons change as we all have different pieces of the puzzle to discover. In the end, we must all rise together and see that this spark that we all possess unites and guides us all. Each journey will look different, the experiences and lessons will differ, but each journey holds valuable insight that is relevant for every spark. Through my own journey I have learned that we are all connected in some way, shape, or form, and because of this connection, we can all benefit from hearing one another's stories and lessons collected along the way. I believe these stories and lessons can have the power to transform our lives and to enlighten us, so we may awaken. With that being said, my journey began a number of years ago, relatively speaking. At 21 years old, some may say the journey is just beginning, but for me, I have been on this path for a long time. It all began when I was 15 years old (more on my personal path later) and has only continued to evolve. The lessons I have learned, wisdom I have received from the Universe, and the experiences I have had as a result of awakening have irrevocably changed me for the better. I continue to awaken each day through new lessons, guidance, and wisdom I receive. It is my hope that through sharing what I have learned on my journey of awakening, you too will be inspired on your own spiritual journey.

Where does it all begin? Trigger. It is the event or cause that catapults you onto the path that will begin your journey. Everyone has a trigger. A point of no return. A moment in time that changes you completely. It is typically unexpected in its arrival, but it needs to be. This moment is set to change our lives; it marks our journey, and it is our job to take the opportunity to learn, to grow, and to follow the plan laid out before us. If we allow it, this trigger will begin to awaken us. It will be as if you were lying dormant up until this point because suddenly you can see the light. The trigger marks the beginning of a new life. One rich and full of enlightenment, growth, and fulfillment. A life far beyond our wildest dreams. Your trigger is the key to a journey that is sure to awaken and enlighten you, but ultimately, you must use the key to unlock the door and take that first step. What happens after the trigger is magical, different for all of us, yet similar in design. We will all learn, grow, and see beyond what we thought was capable, for there is a Divine maestro orchestrating this symphony, and the music is purely brilliant.

A few examples of triggers could be an accident, a birth, a death, a divorce, an illness, or just about any other unexpected or powerful event that provides you with the opportunity to go one of two ways; down a road where you do not change and life remains somewhat stationary, or down a road where everything changes and you live a life rich in meaning. The choice is yours. After all, a trigger is just that, a trigger. You must decide whether or not you will allow it to become the catalyst to change your course. You have the power to transform a trigger into a journey, and when you choose the latter option by allowing your trigger to open you and change your trajectory, your awakening begins.

As the trigger unlocks the path that is your journey, a lot happens that cannot be seen, but is certainly felt. Many of the changes occur internally. It is as if layer by layer, you are removing what no longer serves you as you usher in a new level of awareness and life that is perfect for you. For all the aspects that must be changed, something far greater replaces them. You cannot begin to imagine how impactful a trigger is until you have traveled some distance. You will see that your trigger really does mark your life before the journey and your new life on the journey. There is a disparity because the deeper you go, the more you learn and the more you awaken. As a result, you make more changes, and they tend to run deep. As you begin to awaken and shed your old skin, solitude provides a refuge where clarity can reach you. On my own journey, it has been the times of solitude that I have received the most guidance and clarity. It has also been in solitude that I have been made aware of changes that need to be made in my life in order to move forward. Some relationships may need to be reassessed because not everyone is meant to embark on your journey with you. Not everyone will understand the power of awakening, and others may understand but will not fit with the new direction of your life. Know that this is to be expected, but new relationships will be formed that will augment your awakening. Other possible changes include needing a change of scenery, change of career, change of routine, or just about anything else in our life that can cause us to become stuck. Not every change will occur simultaneously; change builds over time as we become ready to accept it. You will find you are led to make changes along the way that help you to be your most authentic self, and in turn become better aligned with your path. While not every change is fun, because sometimes with growth comes pain, in the end, the journey is much more rich and awe-inspiring when you continue to follow your path and awaken. There will be challenging times, as no one is exempt from these moments; there will also be new gifts and opportunities that are sure to inspire and motivate you. The times of unlocking new gifts or being given incredible opportunities makes every challenge worth it. My journey has taken me to places, both literally and figuratively that have changed me completely, and I have discovered gifts within me that I never would have discovered without following my path (more on gifts later). At the moment of your trigger, all you know is that life is about to change, but you cannot begin to imagine in how many wonderful ways it will change. You will see beyond what you thought was possible, you will discover facts about life that will refine your outlook, and you will learn more about yourself and your core being. But first, the journey has twists and turns; it ebbs and flows, and climbs. As a result, you and your life will experience the same. You will reach new heights by following your path, always learning and growing as you blossom into a more awakened version of yourself. Still, it can be challenging and confusing during some of the climbs, but when you reach the top, you can see the light of day. You reach the top more enlightened and energized than before. In between the climbs, you will experience lower points, but this is all part of the plan. You will learn important lessons during these moments, and you may ultimately use them to reach a high. Because the journey is fluid and has no end, you will continue to have your highs and your lows, but what anchors you during each of these times is trusting that there is a Divine plan, and that each step has purpose in your awakening. Just follow your path, and allow your journey to unfold. It is yours, and it is perfect.

∞THE PATH∞

Path

I have been on the path for a number of years.

*I have found that each step brings
greater insight and depth.*

At first, I was doubtful and somewhat fearful too,

But was reassured when I learned something new.

*Each journey is fraught with obstacles and pain,
but with each step forward something is gained.*

A new gift, new perspective, new opportunity,

Propels you forward entirely.

*Each undulation has something to say,
entices you to go deeper in every way.*

And today on the path I am able to see,

*Just how far I have come and
how much I am yet to see.*

∞THE PATH∞

It was after a period of difficulty that I stepped foot onto the path that is my journey. My trigger and story begin somewhat negatively, but I promise you, it will not remain negative for long... After moving to a new state and subsequent new school, I was bullied. The individual was relentless and wanted to tear me down by calling me names and taunting me each day. It was freshman year at an eastern prep school, and I was miserable and feeling somewhat lost. I had never felt this way before because up until this point I had not really experienced any hardship. My life was idyllic; great friends, the best family, incredible experiences, and more. I had much to be grateful for. During the bullying experience, which dragged on for much of the year, I reached a point where I was unsure of what else to do to fix the situation. I, along with my mother, had already spoken with the school on several occasions, but this only made matters worse as they mishandled the situation (they subsequently changed their bullying policy because of my experience). I lost all but one friend because few believed what I was experiencing and how it affected me. In addition, I had a mystery medical condition with my stomach that took me to top doctors around the country for almost two years. Up until this point, I had been perfectly healthy and had barely missed a day of school. No test was identifying the problem, and I was in pain on a daily basis. I tried to pull myself out of this place, but I needed help, so my family and I sought guidance. What happened as a result was purely Divine and was the catalyst for my awakening.

My family had known of a gifted spiritual teacher, and decided that this was the time to reach out for their help. It was a phone call, meant to help me, between my mother and this spiritual teacher that ushered in my awakening. The teacher shed light on a part of me and existence that I was never fully aware of; the realm of light and universal wisdom. I grew up in a household with faith and connection at the core, but what the spiritual teacher provided was different. They spoke about awareness in the deepest sense, and about the light, and how to be open to it all. The spiritual teacher then went on to offer insight into me, like how I am intuitive and how I empath those around me and therefore need to be cognizant of who I allow into my life. At first, I was somewhat skeptical and fearful of what the spiritual teacher relayed and what it all meant, but it resonated with me and sparked a curiosity in me, and I needed to explore these topics more. It was this new and increased awareness that triggered my inner awakening and opened my eyes to an entirely new world where I would discover my own unique gifts and learn lessons and universal truths meant for everyone that have changed my life completely. With an open mind, I began to explore and immediately discover the truth in the messages while also uncovering more about myself and existence with each step forward. As for my health issues, a last ditch effort led me to an allergist which brought to light what top doctors had missed; multiple food allergies. This experience introduced me to alternative medicine as a healing modality, and for the first time in years, I finally found relief. All of the events in my life at this point in time, while seemingly unrelated, were connected. They led me down a different path towards spirituality and wholeness. Through research and remaining open to the journey, my perspective grew immensely. The following chapters will highlight some of the powerful life lessons I have learned on my journey of awakening, in hopes that they may transform and awaken you as well. Whether your journey is just beginning, or you are well on your way, these lessons and perspectives will help you to live in a more awakened state each day, and will teach you how to receive the most from life, so you may reach your full potential. They have certainly done so for me.

To begin, each path is different, as we are all meant to learn and achieve different things, but one aspect remains the same; the journey will awaken you and change you. A wiser and more evolved being will emerge, and you will feel more alive than ever before.

Know you are guided and supported every step of the way by the Universe, and all you must do to begin your journey is have an open mind, and go where you are led. It sounds too simple to be true, but to begin, this is all it takes. The path will not be without its bumps and jogs; there have certainly been trying times on my own journey that have tested my strength, but it is the difficult times that keep you grounded and that give the extraordinary times meaning. Be willing to make changes in your life, be willing to learn new lessons, and perhaps most importantly, follow your truth; other people's ideas about you or what you should be doing only have power if you allow them to.

The journey is deeply personal. Each soul is unique and is meant to experience different aspects of the human experience in order to learn and to gain what their soul needs to accomplish. This is why we all dream different dreams and make different choices. We all come here with different pieces of our souls unlocked which means we have unique gifts and perspectives. The journey continues with the decision to become more aware; more aware of your surroundings, more aware of yourself, more aware of the spiritual that accompanies us all. It is our mission to unlock more pieces of our soul, to awaken, to learn, and to embody it completely. We all have this potential; but <u>we</u> must choose to unlock it.

Before going further, there are a few things about the journey I wish I had known sooner that I believe will make awakening simpler...

1. Our life, everything and everyone in it, is energy. Since everything is energy, it undulates. Just as waves undulate, so too does life. We often find that after our greatest setbacks come our highest peaks. If we look back at our life from the time we were young up until now, we see a pattern emerge. This pattern is: the lowest points connect to the highest points, and the highest points, to the lowest points. Life, and more specifically our journey, follows this pattern of a wave. We can use the energy of these low points to fuel us so we may catapult to the high points. We would not know good or bad individually if we did not experience them collectively. We need a point of reference to truly be grateful for life and its experiences. While on our journey, we will experience many undulations. With each movement, each breaking wave, we learn something new, and add to the energy that is uniquely us. Expect highs as well as lows. A complete journey requires all experiences. When you are feeling overwhelmed, continue to move forward, do not give up; there is purpose in each step. Something incredible will soon be within reach.

2. Each journey has something in common; every resource and lesson we need to get to the next level are waiting for us at the perfect moment. We will not reach them a moment too soon, or a moment too late. Just when you think you are

finished or have learned everything you needed to learn, another opportunity or experience comes along that teaches you something new, or challenges you to apply what you have learned in the past in a new way. We came to earth to have experiences; to learn, to grow, to change. With each new gift mastered or lesson understood, our soul advances, and we reach a new level of spirituality and enlightenment. It is important to remember that part of being on our spiritual journey means merging the physical with the etheric. We must continue to be present and live life on earth while also being connected and aware of the awesomeness that encompasses every atom in the Universe. It is very much a balancing act, but when you are able to align these two states, life flows beautifully (more on how to find balance later).

3. The journey is unique. No two people will have the exact same experiences, nor will they learn the same lessons, or unlock the same gifts. However, we each hold gifts and potential inside of us that need to be unlocked. It is simply a matter of where we are on our journey as to what is unlocked. It is important to remember we are all at different points on our journeys and have different missions. Some of us are born more awakened than others, some missions are more difficult to fulfill than others, but our journeys are our own, and are each uniquely perfect. Our

journeys unfold at different paces and take us different places. This is what makes the human experience so beautiful. We each represent a different piece to the puzzle, one that radiates pure light when the pieces come together. Each piece has its own form that fits faultlessly into the collective form. Do not compare your journey to someone else's journey. Be proud of who you are and where you are at, knowing that you will awaken and grow at the perfect pace for you.

4. While on the journey, it may seem you are heading one way, while really it is just a step meant to lead you somewhere else. Confusing, I know. The Universe is clever and sometimes it leads us differently than how we would imagine. Our minds are so limited when compared to the unbounded and omniscient Universe. It is not possible for us to see all the Universe sees. Know that each step has purpose, and is divine in its own right. Its purpose may just be different from what we initially believed. It is oftentimes not until we have moved forward that we understand the past and the reason for each step. Hindsight offers a unique vantage point that allows us a clear view into the past. Remember when obstacles arise, there is purpose, and while we may not see it at the time, each obstacle and step is leading us to where we need to be.

5. You can experience the extraordinary while still living ordinarily. What this means is you do

not have to quit your life and live in seclusion or silence. For most, setting an intention or awareness is enough to begin to see positive changes. You can continue to live your life while embarking on this journey to greater awareness as you blossom into the being you were always destined to be. This is not to say no changes will need to be made, but your life can continue to be your life. As you travel deeper into the journey, however, you may find that you want to live differently than before as you uncover the spark and potential within. The journey and awakening change you in the best possible ways.

Just as my journey opened with realizations, so too will yours. They propel us forward. Although we will not all unlock the same gifts, or the same lessons, we can almost always gain something from hearing about one another's journeys. The following life lessons, gifts, universal truths, and experiences from my journey can help to support you on your journey where you will unlock your full potential and blossom into the being you were always destined to be.

You will see the terms Universe and universal truth used throughout. For me, the Universe defines God and all other beings of love and light. Universal truths refer to the lessons or ideas from a Higher Power that are profound and are deeply engrained in us all. If these terms do not align with your beliefs or experiences, feel free to insert the terms you are most comfortable with.

∞BELIEVE∞

Pure Belief

When you believe, something wonderful unfolds.

A light emanates from deep within your soul.

It inspires and propels you to travel down your path,

*Discovering and accepting the
truths so inherent and grand.*

The more you believe, the more you will see,

As you travel deeper still,

The Divine will be revealed in everything.

∞BELIEVE∞

Believe. This is perhaps the most important component of the journey. You must believe in something; anything. Whether this be God, a greater good, the Universe, love, whatever is positive that guides the journey for you. Having something bigger than yourself to look to for guidance, support, and answers adds a feeling of security to the journey because you know you are not walking the path alone. Your beliefs shape your experiences as well as your perception, so they have a very profound impact. For this reason, it is paramount that you form your own beliefs as they are the foundation of the journey. It is also possible that your beliefs will change along the way as you learn additional lessons and encounter new experiences. Know this is okay. The journey changes you, and sometimes, this includes your beliefs. As you uncover new information and have new experiences, old beliefs may not adequately support you, but perhaps the new truths you discover will, and as a result, they become a part of your belief system. Lastly, and perhaps most importantly, believe in yourself. If you do not believe in what you are experiencing; what you are learning; what is guiding you; then none of it matters. Nobody else's belief or opinion of you matters more than your own. If you believe in yourself, and you know that the Universe believes in you, the naysayers cannot bring you down. One of my favorite quotes is by Stuart Chase; it is as follows, "For those who believe, no proof is necessary. For those who don't believe, no proof is possible." To me, this quote really signifies what unfolds on the journey. Not everyone will believe. This is their choice. For these individuals, there is not enough proof to make them believe. Do not become consumed by those who do not believe in you or support you. Keep your vibration high by being a person who believes, and choose to surround yourself with those who see in you what you see in yourself. They will help to lift you up, rather than attempt to tear you down.

Also, if you believe, then you truly believe, always. You cannot believe in one instance or only under certain circumstances. If you believe, then it must hold true no matter what. If you do not believe, then no matter what you encounter and what lies inside of you, nothing will be enough to prove it really exists. When you believe, you trust in what you are experiencing. You know that it is real and it is true. The more you believe, the more you allow yourself to trust in your journey, and the more will be revealed to you. You will continue to travel deeper and unlock even greater messages and truths because you allow yourself to see them. You put yourself in a place where you can experience them. If you constantly question your experiences and choose to believe none of it is real, you will not be able to see the truth because there will be no way to prove to you it is real. You will live in a state where nothing is ever enough, and you will miss out on the transforming power of experiences on your journey.

What happens when you do believe but then something happens that seems to counter what you thought to be true? Were you wrong? Sometimes you may receive guidance or have just gotten a lesson when all of a sudden something happens that seems to unravel it all. It casts doubt on your experiences and lessons you have learned because it causes you to think that maybe you missed the point, or received the message wrong entirely. So, what does it mean? How do you continue from there? I have found that oftentimes you are not wrong. You heard the message correctly. You understood. The journey is multifaceted and you can always learn more or gain more. Sometimes something is placed before you to give you an opportunity to either act on the lesson or to make sure you have truly learned all you needed to learn from it. There are many layers to lessons, and they are often peeled back when we least expect them. I have had times where I will have just learned a new lesson, say on letting go, and I know this lesson to be true, but I encounter a situation that I find myself holding on to, and it is nearly impossible to let go. I cannot suddenly decide that the lesson of letting go was not true or real, or that I am no longer supposed to work to let things go just because my resolve is being tested. As a result, I say that I will work harder to let that which no longer serves me go. I must continue to believe in the message and the purpose, and work to apply it always. You will not always master a lesson right away, some lessons take more time for us to embody completely. If confusion remains, I have found you probably have to go deeper to uncover another layer of the message that you are meant to understand.

When we happen upon these moments, we cannot give up and feel like since one piece did not turn out the way we thought that all subsequent lessons, gifts, or guidance will be wrong as well. We must stay positive and continue to believe. Our journey is taking us in the right direction. We are learning all we are meant to learn when we are meant to learn it. So long as you believe, you will continue to see. There is much we are yet to uncover.

As humans, we have an intrinsic desire to understand the world around us. Most are more comfortable if their surroundings may be quantified and explained. However, there are certain aspects of the Universe, and of our world, that are not meant to be understood. Rather, they must be felt through experience. It is through experience that we are able to begin to understand our world, and even after certain experiences, we are still unable to articulate them. Some phenomenons are just so profound that as humans, we do not possess the words or equations to properly define them. We must accept the fact that not everything is meant to be understood on a physical level, but it may be understood on an emotional or spiritual level beyond our consciousness and comprehension. This is all part of the journey and of believing. There is much to be discovered.

∞LIGHT∞

What is the Light?

It is aglow, it warms the soul,
Gentle in its presence.

It is everywhere yet nowhere,
A palpable force invisible to the eye.

It protects and guides the wandering soul,
Emitting itself every step of the way.

It has no bounds; it is found
Both near and far away.

It never dies; it will always shine
And show the way.

It is The Force, the only force
That illuminates in this way.

This is the Light.
The Source of life.

∞LIGHT∞

What is the light? The word itself conjures up a multitude of thoughts and images. Warmth, happiness, security, love, goodness, positivity. In the case of spirituality and awareness, the light is all of these things as well as the guiding force in our lives. The light is nothing physical in this case; it is invisible yet palpable. It is present in every atom of the Universe; it is the Universe. It surrounds everyone and everything. We all possess the light, and when we project it, it has the power to change reality. How? Light creates more light. You cannot hope to experience greater positivity if you approach life negatively. You cannot will the world to become more loving and awakened if your thoughts and actions are malicious and unilluminated. Your predominant thoughts and actions will affect not only your life, but the lives of everyone else because this is the energy that will be created and distributed. Be the light and others will follow. The concept of light is the nucleus of the entire journey that is awakening. Light is behind all of the good in the world and in ourselves. Without light, we could not physically exist.

We need light to sustain us, to guide us, and to protect us. To understand the strength and significance of light, and to acknowledge and share our inner light propels us in our quest to greater enlightenment and awakening.

Now for how to put the concept of light into practice for palpable results... To project light and to create more light, you must remember a couple of points. First, treat yourself as the being of Light that you are. Be gentle and kind to yourself, focusing on positivity rather than negativity. Next, treat others with this same respect. We are all beings of Light, and should be treated this way. Be kind, be patient, be of service. All of these qualities help the light within ourselves and within others to grow. The sooner we realize the power we hold within, the sooner we can create a new reality and experience a more massive awakening. What this awakening will result in is people loving and accepting other people. Peace as the first step instead of war. Connection over isolation. Enlightenment and truth instead of deceit and lies. This new reality will be born from pure intentions. The light is pure and carries with it a very high, positive vibration. To attract this same energy into our lives, we must, therefore, be pure in our intentions which means our thoughts and actions must be a result of truly wanting to help one another so that we may all experience the light. When you come from a place of light, one where goodness and positivity are central, you will attract more of these things into your life. This corresponds to the power of attraction. If you want to receive greater positivity and light, put greater positivity and light out into the world. Let your approach be one of light.

Light does not have to remain a distant and esoteric concept. If we allow it, the light will assist us to awaken and to create more light so that the whole world may awaken as well. First, light helps to guide us on our journey, gently nudging us in the right direction. How does this manifest? Light in the more literal sense is warm, and in the more etheric case as well; light is warm. If you take a moment to center yourself and breathe, focusing on your core, you can feel the sensation of peace and a sense of warmth. This is the light. It is accessible to you always. All you must do is relax, and set your intention to connect with this light. Now, when you question what decision is best for you in any situation, or which path you should follow, take a moment to become aware of this space within yourself; set your intention to feel the light. Focus on your physical body as you can feel the sensation of light become stronger when considering the right move. This is how the light guides us. When we become aware of our truth and the right answer, we quite literally feel the light. I, personally, make an effort to connect with the light within always, but especially when I have an important decision to make. It is through this method described above that I found the courage to follow my own path in life; I could feel the presence of the light when envisioning this possibility. By following this direction, I am not only more happy and at peace, but I am also awakening more rapidly.

Once conscious of the light, we become aware of the need to share it with the world. It is such an intense and unparalleled experience, you want other people to experience the same. As we all know, one spark can start a fire, and when we consciously project light, we ignite the light in others as well. An awakening can happen when people operate from a place of light because each individual sparks change in another until everyone is awake. If we embody the light wholeheartedly, others will follow suit and the world will be enveloped by light. Before this can happen, we must realize that in order to create widespread change, we must change ourselves first. This means we must practice embodying the light in our own lives, going on our own journeys, and taking action that will generate more light.

A final thought. The light is stronger than any force of darkness we may encounter. Darkness dissolves into a shadow when light shines more brightly. Light may be used to transmute darkness and negativity into light. In fact, it is the only way to eradicate these forces because light creates more light. Any time we face darkness or get bogged down by negativity, inviting the light into our lives lessens its hold. In time, as we fuel the light, and shine our personal light, the darkness will become a mere shadow and the light will cast a protective glow on the world.

∞GUIDANCE∞

Guidance

Their melody guides us when we are in tune,

Creating a harmony when we
listen and follow through.

Trust that their guidance reveals the truth,

As we seek their knowledge,

The answers will come through.

∞LISTEN∞

Listen. This was my first moment of enlightenment. Such a simple word and action. We all do it everyday, right? We listen to conversations around us, to directions given to us, to constant noise and chatter. They consume us. However, this is not the listening I am referring to. The listening I am referring to is perhaps the most significant form of listening; the voice within. Everyday we receive messages and guidance from the Universe and/or Divine, but we fail to recognize them because our focus is on the everyday events of life. We forget to listen to ourselves and to the Universe; the voices that hold our truth. In other words, we let the noise of our outer environment, drown the wisdom of our inner environment. We allow the chatter and distractions from everyday life to be all we hear, which makes us miss out on all of the wisdom that becomes apparent only when it is quiet enough to hear it. When you begin to truly listen to what is important; allowing your inner voice and the Universe to be the compass guiding you to a higher place, the perfect opportunities, experiences, and advice find you. That problem you had that needed a solution, the perfect contact to get you a new job, or the direction to take to live your dreams. All of the answers come when you listen and are quiet enough to hear them.

How do you listen, and how do you know you are receiving a message? First, you listen which requires you silence your outer environment by removing any distractions. Then, you must quiet your inner environment, which admittedly takes some practice. For many of us, our minds never stop; we are always thinking about or worrying about something. But, in order to receive the messages and wisdom that we seek, our minds must be silent. Try closing your eyes, taking deep breaths, and focusing your attention inward. Pay attention to how you feel physically, what your emotions are telling you, and take note of any thoughts, words, images, or feelings that come to you. When you are in this space, you are connecting with and listening to your inner voice which is connected to the Universe and to the Divine. Try this exercise for a few minutes daily; you will see results. An important reminder when listening for Divine guidance relates to distorting the messages. Many times while we wish to receive Divine guidance, we also wish to hear what we want to hear. As a result, our minds can sometimes interfere with the message and distort it. If the truth is what you seek, and you want guidance that will benefit and help you, then you cannot listen to your own judgements, desires, or opinions. Instead, you must turn your filter off and listen to the wisdom and voice of the Universe. When you enter into the space to receive Divine guidance just be sure to set your own thoughts aside so the Divine messages do not become distorted. While you do need to avoid interfering with a message, you do not need to be afraid to pose a question to the Universe. If you need guidance or support, or you have a specific question, send it out to the Universe and be receptive to the response. The answer may come during another moment of quietness, or it may come while you are consumed in a project and paying no attention. Regardless, when it comes, listen.

When you receive a message, you may feel heat radiating from the inside out, you may get chills suddenly, butterflies in your stomach, your sinuses may open, or you may experience a lightbulb moment where you suddenly become aware and have greater clarity. The bottom line is, you will know without a shadow of doubt that you are receiving a Divine message. When it happens, give it the time and attention it deserves. Messages and guidance from the Divine are the most valuable insight you will ever receive, so cherish them. Know that an answer may not seem to come right away, or things may not work out the way you intended them to; do not get discouraged. Despite our greatest efforts, the messages will not come until the time is perfect for us. While this may not fall under our idea of perfect timing, it will be the perfect time according to the Universe. As much as we would all like to, we cannot control when this happens. We must trust that in time all will be revealed, and in the meantime, we just need to open our hearts and listen, being ready to take action when the time comes. Stay open and positive and know that all of the questions will be answered, all of the problems will be solved, and all of the doors will be unlocked when the time is right for you.

When we are out of touch and allow all of the "noise" and distractions around us to drown out the whispers from the Universe, the messages and signals only became louder. This, for me, is the best and most interesting fact of listening to messages. I try very hard to listen carefully and receive messages the first time, but it often takes more than one try to get a message through to me. The first time, I either do not hear the message at all, or I doubt my ability to hear the message accurately, so miss it. Every single time, the message only becomes louder, and the delivery more creative, until I finally receive the message loud and clear. Listening and receiving messages from the Universe is not an exact science; it is something that takes continual effort, but once you hear from the Universe, your world opens and changes before you as the words have a power all their own. Thankfully, if you miss the message the first time the Universe continues to try to get through to you. Can you imagine if we only received a message once, and if we missed it, the opportunity passed? You have plenty of opportunities to receive a message. When you really need to hear it, the Universe finds a way to reach you. Just be open to them and trust what you hear.

∞GUIDANCE∞

Guidance. It is how the Universe converses with us, and it comes in countless forms. Friends, family, a perfectly timed message, situation, stranger, or perhaps directly from above. However it finds us, and yes, guidance finds us whether we are seeking it or not, has the potential to be profound when embraced. When we need help, regardless of if we consciously ask for it or not, the Universe sends us messages through guidance to show us the way. It may come as an answer to a prayer, the perfect song at the perfect moment on the radio, a billboard flashing a message, a conversation overheard, or a feeling in our gut. However the guidance comes, it is intended to support us and to encourage us. It comes at just the right moment in time and when acknowledged, cannot be mistaken. It rings true in our soul. We have all received guidance at some point because we are all guided throughout our journey, whether we ask to be or not. We cannot walk the path alone; we need the Universe to show us which direction to take. There are many moving parts to the journey, and we would become overwhelmed by them if left to our own devices. We need guidance to bring clarity and wisdom to us so we may make the best choices. While we need guidance, the language of the Universe is, at times, complex because it can come in countless forms. Sometimes guidance requires reflection before all will be revealed. Other times, its message is clear from the beginning. It may not come as words, it will not always be audible, but it will always be palpable. We have all had those moments when chills are sent down our spine, or the hair on our arms stands straight up because whatever was said or experienced is somehow connected to us. Maybe as you seek an answer or need assistance, you get a "gut" feeling or feel your heart "tug." Dreams are another common way for the Universe to communicate with us. When we sleep and dream, our conscious minds take a break, and we may more easily receive messages from the spiritual realm because we are not analyzing and judging the information. Dreaming allows us to access a wealth of wisdom by connecting to the Source. When we awaken, we may recall our dreams and find we received great assistance for our journey.

All of the above examples of feelings, dreams, or reactions can be guidance. This is why reflection may be necessary. When you meditate on how you feel or the details of an encounter or situation, guidance comes to light and the pieces fall into place. Depending upon how guidance finds us, we may not always consciously remember the details, but the essence of the message remains intact. When we reflect on the encounter, we are able to remember more details and piece together the messages and guidance. While at times the guidance may not make sense, trust that in time it will and that it is leading you to where you need to be. The Universe is never wrong; trust in its Divine nature.

There is a very important lesson on guidance and that is where it comes from. The guidance I am referring to throughout is guidance from a benevolent force of love and light that is positive in its approach and direction. When you receive guidance you should feel good, warm and fuzzy, if you will. Guidance from this force will never make you feel bad or tell you to harm yourself or anyone else. If you receive guidance of this kind, promptly wrap yourself in a blanket of light, and ask that this energy be defeated. Remind yourself to only connect to the good by saying a mantra, "I only listen to and receive guidance from the highest order of Light Beings." This will help you to reconnect with this positive energy. When guidance emanates from this force, its aim is to help guide you in the right direction, and to help you navigate through different choices you have to make or challenges you must endure. Guidance of this kind will not only make you feel great, but it will also move you in the right direction.

As humans, we oftentimes favor relying upon logic to dictate the choices we make, or the direction we go. However, with guidance and the Universe, you cannot use logic how we tend to use logic because the logic of the Universe is different from our idea of logic. There are connections that exist between things that we cannot see, but we can oftentimes feel them. Even though we cannot always see the connection, the Universe can. The connection the Universe knows of makes the guidance logical. In the meantime, we tend to believe our feelings are irrational. Why can the Universe see connections we cannot? It goes back to the overall plan or blueprint for our lives. While we do not possess the plans, which leaves us somewhat in the dark, the Universe does. As a result, the Universe sees how every step and piece of guidance fits together. As a result, if you feel there is something you must do, or a direction you must go; that you are being led by a force greater than yourself, you must follow it. If not, you may miss out on something great. The Universe knows the right steps for you, and even if guidance does not make sense to us, there is always a connection. If you feel it strongly, follow it, because guidance is only effective when listened to. The Universe offers you guidance daily, but a lot of times, we are too preoccupied to notice. We must be in tune with ourselves and listen to our feelings as this is how the Universe tends to guide us. Once we establish how we feel, we can then follow the guidance and travel in the direction we are being led. Free will is a factor in whether or not guidance is successful. If we choose not to heed the guidance we are given, and instead ignore it and maybe even do the opposite, we cannot be upset when things do not work out. I have learned that when you receive guidance from the Universe to listen to it and follow it even if it does not make sense at the moment. Sometimes, you are being given a heads up for an event to come, and you need certain information in advance to help you make the right decision in that moment.

An example of guidance that outwardly seems irrational, but was actually Divine guidance comes in the form of a story from someone I once coached. This person found themselves stuck in a rut in their current job and environment and felt they really needed a change. Logic would dictate they would either find a new job in their current location or find a different job in a new location. However, neither of these options felt right. Instead, this person received Divine guidance in the form of a strong feeling that they needed to move to a different state they were drawn to even though they did not have a job offer or logical reason to move there. This change would mean uprooting their life, but they felt it was what they were being guided to do. This person listened to this guidance, moved, and as soon as they did, everything came together, they felt at peace, and have since been more successful and happier than ever before, in more ways than one. Evidently, in this case, and many more like this one, logic could not explain what the Universe knew. There was a connection that our logic missed. For whatever reason, this person needed to make a change and they landed where they needed to be. If this person had based their decision on pure logic, they would have missed out on an incredible experience.

Another example is a personal one. As my journey has continued, I have learned time and time again to listen to the guidance I receive, but when my journey was just beginning, this was more difficult. After the bullying experience I had as a freshman in high school, I made the difficult, and seemingly irrational decision to attend the remainder of high school online. This decision meant I would not be in school with friends and have a more traditional experience that most desire. I knew that this decision would take me down a different path that may have more challenges, like isolation, but something in me (Divine guidance) led me to go down the path less traveled. It is this decision that really cemented the journey for me. After attending the remainder of high school online, I graduated a year early, began college online immediately, graduated college in under three years, and began my spiritual work. Had I not made this seemingly illogical decision, I am sure I would not be here today writing this book, helping others on their own spiritual journeys. Without that isolation and time to reflect, I would not have received the wisdom that I did, nor would I have awakened in the way that I have. As you can see, I received Divine guidance that took me down a completely different path than I had been on, and realistically would have continued on. I am grateful that I listened to my gut. My life has turned out better than I could have imagined, and while aspects of this decision have come with challenges, I would not trade it for anything. This is why even if a decision seems irrational in the traditional sense, it can make perfect sense from the perspective of the Universe. I encourage you to take more into account than traditional logic when making your decisions, especially the life changing ones. Listen to the guidance you receive. It can change your life completely... For the better.

∞TRUST∞

Trust

Trust in the blueprint,

The image for life.

Trust its directions are perfectly aligned.

The Higher Power holds all the plans

And only reveals them

When we can...

Trust in their source, and purpose too.

Make a promise to

Follow them through.

The plans and directions are from the Divine,

Therefore, we must trust

They are perfectly timed.

∞TRUST∞

If you are to embark on this journey, which at this point, has most likely been decided, then you must remember to trust. If you are anything like me, you probably prefer to be in control. This is your comfort zone and you can dictate where you go. However, this is not how the journey works. While you always have free will, you, like me, will quickly learn that you are not captain of this ship. The Universe is. You cannot control every experience, lesson, and direction the journey may bring your way. This is why you must learn to trust. Many times along the journey you will feel as though your direction is unclear because the pieces will not seem to fit. From experience, they always do, we just do not see how. We must trust in the big picture and know there is a plan beyond our comprehension and control, and continue to follow the steps even if they do not currently make sense to us because there is a purpose whether or not we see it. Much of the journey involves a realm beyond our consciousness which means that we will oftentimes encounter points and events that while occurring within our consciousness, are actually derived from beyond our consciousness. More simply, we only see one fragment of what is actually occurring in our Universe at one time. As a result, much is beyond our knowing which causes some confusion for us when we experience the times that do not seem to fit. Our vantage point does not offer the clearest view. The Universe, however, has a front row, unobstructed view of everything. This is why we must trust that the Universe knows what we cannot fathom, and that despite how it may appear, we are in fact moving forward, and the journey is unfolding perfectly. It can be difficult when the events in your life seem to point towards one direction, but they do not add up to what you feel or what you want. Even during these times, more so perhaps, you have to trust that you are aligned to the plan for your life, and you are continuing to move forward on your journey. While we may not see how these events connect to the bigger picture, they always do.

Here is a personal example. At the start of my journey, I thought that because I was awakening, I would not experience the same hardships as others who were not awake. I thought I was somehow exempt. This notion was shattered when difficulties arose like feeling a lack of direction in my life, being lonely, and having health issues, et cetera. I could not see how these experiences fit into the big picture, until I had a realization. Awakening did not mean I was exempt from human experiences, that I would never encounter any difficulties ever again; what awakening meant was viewing these experiences as an opportunity to practice positivity, to learn life lessons, and to trust in God's plan. In hindsight, I can see that my "lack of direction" was because it was not time for me to know my purpose. My loneliness was meant for me to grow spiritually, and to collect lessons that were to be shared later on. My health issues were meant for me to see that the physical body is connected to the spirit, and negativity eventually manifests itself physically. I also needed to align my physical body with my spiritual awakening, which meant changing my diet to be more healthful. As I continued to awaken, I also had the realization that these "difficulties" were also the catalysts that triggered my journey, so there was a profound purpose within them all. The bottom line is, every event and experience is tied to the overall plan for your life, and while sometimes in the moment you cannot see it, there is a reason for everything. Trust in the direction of your life and journey, that you are on your path to becoming who you were always intended to be. There may be times where you just want to give up because you cannot see how all of the pieces fit together, and from your vantage point it looks as though you are moving backward rather than forward, but just continue to trust. The journey moves us forward into the future. The past may be used as a tool to learn, but the journey itself and the direction you follow is one of forward motion. In addition, you may experience moments of anxiety when you cannot see what comes next on the journey; I know I certainly have, but you must remember and trust that in the end all will be as it is meant to be. It may look different from what we had imagined, but it will always turn out the way it is supposed to. Being skeptical is oftentimes easier than trusting, but you will be shown in many different ways that trusting will get you to where you need to be.

Courage

There will come times that will test our strength,

But we must show courage and maintain our faith.

Our capabilities extend farther
and deeper than we know.

Our tenacity and courage will certainly show.

We must resolve to move forward

Courageously,

As the journey is difficult, yet rewarding;

We will see.

∞COURAGE∞

It takes courage to embark on a journey. A journey of awakening is no different. You have to face the unknown, taking each step without knowing for certain where the journey leads. At times this can be frightening because you feel a loss of control. If you are not in control, then who is? What you have to remember is the Universe is your guide and if you take a leap of faith and follow the path before you, the Universe will support you. You are not alone on this journey; there is a Divine force walking alongside of you. It can be difficult to trust this is the case when you cannot see this force, but with courage must come faith, and you must have faith not only in the journey itself, but also in who or what is guiding the journey. No matter how difficult life may become, or how many trials and tribulations you may face, you must always keep the faith if you wish to reach the other side. Faith can provide the support and encouragement needed to carry on by infusing meaning into any situation and by providing hope and purpose. When you have faith that everything happens for a reason and that you are being taken care of, the gravity of a situation becomes much lighter. Sometimes faith is all we have, and it is important to make every effort to maintain it. It makes the bad times easier and the good times greater. With courage and faith you can overcome any obstacle in your path and find the strength to continue on.

The steps throughout the journey can be both intimidating and rewarding because while the idea of accomplishing certain steps is enough to make you want to quit now, they allow for intense growth and enjoyment as well. Whether this involves a new business, a move, ending a relationship, or any other difficult decision, in these moments if you choose to display courage and have faith, you are able to experience that growth and enjoyment. Allowing fear to creep in only prevents you from being courageous and causes you to miss out on a potentially fantastic opportunity. In moments when the fear begins to take over because it inevitably will, ask the Universe to help you; to bring forth your courage. Simply ask for help. It is often already within you, but sometimes you need help in bringing it out.

It is with courage that we navigate through life's challenges. Challenges can be fun and rewarding if channeled correctly. I view challenges as having opportunity. They can bring enlightenment, change, growth, even success. Some challenges are actually a springboard that help you to reach your destination faster. They can cause you to take on a new perspective or think outside of the box which leads to breakthroughs.

There is also value in challenges partially because success is sweeter when you have had to overcome obstacles and work hard to get there. I would not feel the same amount of fulfillment if I simply landed wherever I wanted to go without putting forth any effort. When you encounter a perceived challenge, try to see how you could leverage it to actually make it work in your favor and propel you forward. Stay positive, focus on your goal, do not back down. Some challenges are a gift.

In addition, if there is ever any other quality you would like to embody, or one that you feel needs some attention, ask for it. Sometimes you are given that quality in the moment for a situation or time you are going through, but other times the Universe will provide you with the opportunity or situation to help you develop the quality and truly embody it through your actions. Regardless, really make an effort to put these qualities to use, so they may assist you each time along the way you need to call upon them. As these opportunities arise, know that the Universe is there to support you and guide you. While it takes time to realize, you have far greater capabilities than you are aware of. Sometimes the situations that require the most courage and faith have the tendency to bring these capabilities to the surface. When you exemplify courage through a difficult situation, you may find you are stronger than you believed and that you have less fear going forward because you triumphed in the end. When you continue to be courageous and have faith, not allowing the dark times to bring you down, you will find going forward you have a greater sense of strength and peace because you remained standing. This greater perspective carries through and permeates all areas of your life. Suddenly, you will find it takes a lot more to rattle you, and you are better equipped to handle the low points. I believe we all have a latent inner power and tenacity that may be summoned in challenging times. We all have light within us, that spark of Divinity I have mentioned before. This spark holds a tremendous amount of power, and when we set the intention to connect with this piece of ourselves, and to use it, it expands. As a result, this spark, with all of its brilliant power, gives us the strength we need to face our challenges, whatever they may be. Acknowledge the light within. Use it so it may shine brilliantly. The darkness and challenges will begin to fade because the light transforms them.

A time when I needed to find courage was in writing this book and sharing my journey. I tend to be more private and I feared judgement if I opened myself up. However, I knew I was being led down this path for a reason, and in order to help others, I needed to share my journey too. I put my faith in the Divine, found courage, and took the first step. This initially meant sharing my story with a select few, and then branching out to others who I knew had similar beliefs to my own. Slowly, I opened up, and now while I still have some uneasiness, I am much more comfortable presenting my authentic self to the world. While there will continue to be obstacles, with courage, I will confidently move forward.

∞LEARN∞

Learn

We are all students yearning to learn

All of the messages there are to discern.

While on earth, the journey is meant to help
us build upon what we already know,

And continue to live, learn, and grow.

As beings of Light, we must come to
see, being awakened is the key.

The journey is fluid, the lessons run deep,

So, as students, we must continue to be.

∞LEARN∞

Learning is a major motif throughout the journey. In a sense, it is the journey. As you learn, meaning is bestowed upon your experiences. Learning helps you to awaken because it unlocks pieces of your soul as you uncover the lessons and truths meant to help you grow. It is what allows you to become enlightened, have greater meaning revealed, and advance. I should mention that when I discuss learning, I do not mean learning math or a language. While these subjects are incredibly important, learning as it pertains to the journey is in a spiritual sense. There is a great deal to learn and we are never really finished. There is always a level above, or a step deeper that could be explored. On this journey that we are currently living on earth, we will only travel so far. Not everything is meant to be understood now or even in this lifetime. Even so, there are numerous lessons we must master in this lifetime in order to further unlock our souls. There are even lessons about lessons! A few that I have learned along the way are as follows...

Lessons are infinite, it seems you learn a new one with each turn. You will reach them when you need to learn them, not necessarily when you are ready to understand them or accept them. The interesting aspect of lessons are they will continue to come around until we understand them, accept them, and act upon them. This means that if at first you miss the point, you will be given more opportunities to learn the lesson in new ways, until you glean what you need to from it. It is not a case where if you miss it once, you miss it forever, or that your journey will be completely halted until you figure it out. The journey will continue, you will simply be given other lessons until the timing and proper opportunity comes about for you to try the lesson again. It should also be said that you are never finished learning. There is no magic point you reach where suddenly you have learned all there is to know. You will always be able to dig deeper, uncover more, or understand a lesson differently. For those of us who appreciate closure or who yearn to complete something entirely before moving on, it may be difficult because the journey does not always unfold in this way. Learning is asynchronous. Life is considerably richer when you allow yourself to learn whenever the lessons arise.

It is not just the awareness of a lesson, it is the action. You can understand a lesson completely and accept it on some level, but until you act on the lesson, you have not completely embraced it. Action, for me, is one of the more difficult steps. It is easier to learn and evolve, accepting the lessons along the way, but to actually put them into practice takes presence and effort. You must consciously remind yourself to apply the lessons you have learned to your life and change your actions to reflect greater knowledge. You must act. Without action, truths and lessons are left to collect dust in your mind while your outer environment remains the same. With action, truths and lessons remain active in your mind, and your reality changes because you live the lessons and embody them. This is the moment when you have truly learned the lesson and achieved it. When you take action, not only will you advance, but others will take note as well, and they too may learn and advance. Learning promotes learning. The cycle continues infinitely. While the topic is one that is fairly basic and straightforward, it is also powerful and profound, shaping our experiences and touching our souls. Its impact on us and our lives is unmistakable and bold.

Truth

*The truth comes as a feeling, it
resonates deep in your soul.*

A powerful reminder of all there is to know.

*Whether it comes to you in slumber
or you hear it from a sage,*

*The truth touches you in such a way,
you know it is no mistake.*

It seems as if it has come from beyond this plane.

*The truth comes as a feeling, reminding
you of all there is to know.*

The true wisdom, lies within your soul.

∞TRUTH∞

The Universe holds an infinite number of truths. These truths plant a seed that sprouts an awakening not just through one person, but through many. These truths provide knowledge and wisdom from the heart of the Universe, where everything spiritual resides, so when we receive this knowledge in any form, it leads to spiritual growth and advancement. Universal truths hold tremendous power because we all may awaken from them. A universal truth for one is a universal truth for all. They unite us because they are spiritual fact. This is why when you hear a universal truth, it resonates with you. Somewhere beneath the surface, you know it is the truth, and it reawakens you. They tend to be more etheric in nature and are difficult to articulate, partially because they are limitless. Also, a universal truth is oftentimes already within your soul, dormant; but when you encounter it again, it becomes activated, leading you to growth and spiritual advancement. In a sense, universal truths are affirmations. We have heard many truths before, whether in this plane or another, but we cannot consciously access them on command, the reason being our souls retain this knowledge and many of us are not able to connect effortlessly with our souls while our conscious minds are active. We know a lot more than we can consciously recall at any moment in time. Much of our knowledge is locked away beneath the surface for us to rediscover at a later time. This is part of the journey to awakening; to discover the power and wisdom that is already within us. When we once again receive a universal truth, it affirms what we already knew on a deep, soul level. Universal truths hold immense power because they allow us to experience a richer perspective through them. Our world views, connection to one another, even the journey itself, are all shaped by the universal truths we encounter. They are gifts from the Universe as they offer vast insight from the depths of the Universe to the depths of our souls. They connect us to our spiritual home by bringing a piece of it here to our physical world and challenging us to delve deeper into ourselves and the wisdom we encounter on our quest to awakening.

One example of a universal truth to illustrate its effect is love is light, and light is love. In order for there to be love, there must be light and positivity. In order for there to be light, then there must be love. This is perhaps the greatest way to spread light, through love. Love yourself, love one another, love the Universe. This emotion and action connects us back to the Divine power that created us by awakening that spark within ourselves and within one another. You will encounter other spiritual truths within this book and through your experiences on your own journey too. When you encounter them, you will know what you have discovered because you will feel it completely with every fiber of your being, to the depths of your soul.

A universal truth or lesson finds you when it is time for you to know it or learn it. It could come to you seemingly randomly as a thought or a feeling, almost as if a switch was flipped. Or, it could come after you seek assistance or answers to a problem or situation in your life. A sage may impart a truth unto you, a friend may say something that clicks, or you may have a profound dream. There is no limit to the number of ways a truth may find you because the vessel it comes in is not what is most important. It is the message, the truth itself, that matters the most. This is why when the truth finds you, you will know because when you hear it, it resonates deeply. The hairs on your arms may stand up, you may get chills, or feel a surge of energy rush through you. It may even bring you to tears. I have experienced all of the above. The truth reaches your heart, and your heart speaks to you in feelings, which are its language, so you feel messages that are of the heart and of the soul. The truth comes from beyond our plane of reality, and when it is spoken, your soul recognizes its origins. The connection is powerful. Our souls need the truth to awaken and to become enlightened on the journey. When we find the truth, speak the truth, and live our truth, the energy we send out is positive and powerful. We awaken.

∞ENERGY∞

Undulations

Pressure builds, I can't see that which surrounds me.

I can't hear the Voice

As well as when

I'm free falling.

And then, I hear the Voice

Ring clear as a bell

Awaken me,

When suddenly,

I see that which surrounds me.

I hear the Voice that speaks to me.

No pressure, just air,

As I rise to begin again...

∞ENERGY∞

Energy. How do you articulate something that the physical eyes cannot see? Even though the eyes cannot see energy, it can certainly be perceived, and we experience the effects of energy all of the time. All energy is, is a series of vibrations. These vibrations determine our reality. It sounds simple, and in some ways it is. When a vibration is created in the span of a second, our environment is signaled to respond accordingly. For the purpose of the journey, there are a couple of types of vibrations that generally effect our reality. They are classified as either being positive or negative. What determines the type of vibration that is created? Thoughts, feelings, words, and actions. Sending out good thoughts and feelings creates positive energy, while sending out negative or hateful thoughts and feelings creates negative energy. With each, a wave, or vibration is created. As a result of the two forces interacting, there are highs, there are lows, and there are places in-between; we experience them all. Our own energy sends out vibrations to our surroundings that then sends back to us what we put out, like a feedback loop. It is all energy, and you have the power to change it. By changing the vibrations you emit, you change not only your energy, but the energy around you. In turn, your reality and experience becomes congruent with your predominant energy. If you are not pleased with the tone of your reality, send out a new, more positive vibration. The changes will be noticeable because your environment will align itself accordingly. Now for the complex part of energy. As different vibrations intermix, a new vibration is formed. Think of it as mixing colors. If you take blue and yellow and mix them together, a new color, green, is created. This new color has properties of both blue and yellow, but has its own as well. The same is true of vibrations interacting. This new energy carries with it traits from all of the vibrations before, which allows for an unlimited number of possibilities. Ultimately, only one possibility will become reality. This is why our energy is so important. It helps to determine which reality we will face at this point in time. The more positive vibrations you emit, the greater the chance of experiencing positive outcomes because there are more positive vibrations interacting. Even so, on our journeys, there will be times of great positivity, and times of negativity. It is part of deciding to embark on the journey. No matter what situation you may find yourself in, you have the power to change the energy surrounding both you and the situation. Positive energy has tremendous effects on everything. When you choose to emit positive energy by both being positive outwardly as well as inwardly with your perception, your environment will become more positive as well. You will attract more positive things into your life because of the space you have created. If you find yourself in a negative place more often than not, you will experience more events of this kind enter your life. Again, you cannot be negative but expect to see positive results. This simply does not work. You experience what you choose to be and what you choose to see, so if you are only negative, you will see, feel and experience negativity as well. Projecting negativity, whether deliberate or not, will lower the vibration of you and your surroundings which is why negativity breeds negativity. Even when the Universe throws us a curveball, we can approach it from a positive perspective and learn from it, thus attracting positive things. However, if we allow ourselves to be brought down by negativity, then we attract more of the same. I learned this lesson the hard way. Whenever I viewed something as being negative, I could actually feel a heaviness descend upon me. It was like I was being sucked down a hole and the further down I went, the less light I could see. This is not a pleasant feeling, so over time, I learned to make an effort to see the good and stay above it all, focusing on being positive. When I approached life this way, I could actually feel myself getting lighter, and a fog was lifted from my mind, offering more clarity. From that point on, I have made a conscious effort to maintain a positive outlook no matter what obstacles I may face. It not only makes the challenging situation more manageable, but it attracts more positive things to me in the future.

It is important to always look for the positive even when you feel like you are treading in a sea of darkness. Look at that bright spot as if it were a life raft, because it is. Hold on to that positive vision because it will ultimately lead you out of the darkness and into a place of light. If we only focus on how we are being dragged down, and not on how we can get back up, we will forever be stuck in that bottomless sea of darkness... Treading, barely hanging on. But, if we can focus on even one positive in our life, then that sea of darkness is no longer bottomless, but rather becomes a puddle. Now instead of treading, we just need our rain boots. Armed with this realization, the light will be able to take over our life, and pretty soon all we will see is the sunshine and dry pavement.

I know what that sunshine and light feels like. It has warmed my soul, and touched my life. However, in order to get to this place, I had to experience that darkness as well. We all do. In good times as well as bad, I have found something that always helps. Meditation and golden light. Yes, you read correctly. When you meditate, you connect. It does not matter what you connect with so long as it is positive. You only have to meditate for a few minutes a day to begin to see changes. Whether you meditate for five minutes or an hour, meditation or quiet time can help us to see the good even when life seems to be fraught with the bad. When we are centered and focused on the positive, we can then find a way to begin to heal the darkness, so that we may usher in a life filled to the brim with light. The more you are able to focus on the positive, the less darkness is able to have a hold on you. How do you meditate? There is no right or wrong way, it is a matter of personal opinion. Some individuals find a guided mediation to be most beneficial because it allows them to be guided into a more relaxed and centered state. Others find it helpful to listen to soft music or chants to help them get into the proper frame of mind. Some people meditate by sitting silently with their eyes closed, and focus on their breathing and maintaining a clear mind. Others may also pose a question before meditating and then allow the answer to reach them while in this state. There are many helpful books and music specifically designed to support meditating and they can be found in most bookstores. I personally meditate by closing my eyes, and having a conversation with God, asking questions, and listening for a response. I go through everything that I am grateful for, and envelope myself with golden light. This practice grounds me and puts me into a positive space. No matter how you meditate, you should find a quiet space where you can relax, unwind, and remove yourself from all distractions. Close your eyes and take a few deep breaths. Then proceed to follow whatever practice you choose. If you are new to meditation, I would encourage you to try a few different techniques to find what you are most comfortable with. Whatever method works best for you is the correct form.

Another technique that has helped me to remain positive is golden light. Throughout the day and before going to sleep, I envision myself being enveloped in golden light. I imagine this light reaching ever cell in my body, from my head to my toes. I then envision the light surrounding me from around, above my head to beneath my feet. This light is not only within me, but also around me. I view it as an impenetrable bubble that only allows positivity and light in, and keeps darkness out. I draw this light from a reserve of positive energy that can never become depleted. Everyone can access this reserve. Just envision a giant pool of golden light and begin to draw from it, wrapping it around yourself in a clockwise motion as you do so. You will begin to feel protected and at peace. If something happens during the day that is negative, I make sure to continue imagining this golden light around me. You can do the same; there is no limit to how often you can draw from this light. I know this concept sounds crazy, but trust me, it works every time.

These techniques have given me the feeling of never being alone, the feeling of support, and the feeling of unconditional love. I take these feelings with me, and use them as armor to protect me during the day. I began this ritual five years ago, and still use it today. I urge everyone to meditate and to envision the light. Everyone needs to be in a quiet, relaxed state to recharge for a while, and see the world with a fresh set of eyes. Meditation and light cross all religious barriers and connect us with our spiritual side. You do not have to have a particular set of beliefs for these methods to benefit you. So long as you connect with something positive, and feel better as a result, this is all that matters.

The key to it all is we must remain positive to create positive change. Like attracts like. The Universe will give back to us whatever energy or idea we send out. At first, this realization is frightening because when we think back to all of the different thoughts and ideas we have had over time, we probably think "oops..." But, if we put the idea of like attracts like into the present and future tenses, it is reassuring. We have some control over our experiences. By focusing on the positive in a situation, or holding a positive vision for the future, that is what we are attracting for right now. You will find that when you remain positive about a situation, more positive experiences will present themselves now. This is because the positive energy we are sending out is received by the Universe, and given back to us. Imagine a world where everyone sent out positivity and light. Our own lives would change for the better, and so would the lives of billions of others. One small shift in our perspective has the ability to change the world...

Balancing Act

The balancing act comes in to play

As I am reminded everyday

That only pieces of me belong here,
while others belong There.

The balance for me lies in between.

This balancing act goes up and down,

Until I can find a way to keep my feet on the ground.

But even on these days, inevitably,

I find myself soaring high above the trees.

But this is who I am, this is me.

Like a fulcrum on a seesaw, I live in between.

∞BALANCE∞

Balance. Naturally, the physical world, ourselves included, strive for balance. In order to feel most at peace, we must find balance in our lives. It is a spectrum, and is therefore different for everyone. We each have our own set points, or level of balance we need to function optimally and feel at peace. When we become imbalanced in any aspect of our life, the need to restore equilibrium causes it to become balanced again. Typically, the process to correct imbalance is not without difficulty as we become accustomed to the imbalance, so any change creates some level of discomfort. Take work, for example. We view work as good because it often provides purpose and a paycheck. However, today, many find themselves working far too many hours at the expense of time for themselves or their families. This imbalance, while common and mostly accepted, is still imbalance, and naturally, the system must correct itself. This may come in the form of an illness, loss of a job, or any other event that forces you to take a step back and reallocate your time. Yes, this process would be uncomfortable and stressful at first, but in the end, the balance you experience will bring about calm and peace. I have seen this unfold time and time again. Although it may seem as though this experience would be terrible at first, when you remove the stressors and causes of imbalance, the path is cleared for greater things, and there is space and time for more in your life that matters. The initial discomfort and even strife eventually leads to greater peace.

On the opposite end of the balance spectrum are things like friends, travel, luxuries, and food. More is better, many say. How can you have too much of a good thing? It can be challenging to make certain changes even if balance results because we do not view all imbalance as bad, like in the above instances. If these "good things," which in the right amount are indeed very good, become too all consuming, your life becomes imbalanced and you begin to have these things at the expense of something else. Too much time with friends, not enough time to reflect and learn. Too much travel, not enough rest to recharge. Too many luxuries, disconnection. Too much food or indulgences, illness and disease. You get the idea. We need balance to thrive, and while the optimal balance is different for everyone, we all have a range of ideal balance that we must discover for ourselves.

It must also be noted that balance does not mean perfection. Perfection does not exist, not on earth anyway. While the Universe functions at perfection, the human piece on earth prevents us from functioning the same. We have free will, and make our own decisions, which at times means we stray from the plan and our path. We find our way back, just in a different way than initially intended at times. The human factor, with our free will and propensity for intense emotion, also means that our actions have ripple effects on everyone else on earth, so no matter which direction we go, or which choice we make, someone, somewhere will feel the effects. This is both good and bad. If our actions are well intentioned and kind, others feel and receive this kindness; but if our actions are malicious, others receive this too. It is because of these dualities that we experience imbalance, or imperfection, negativity and positivity. All of this is part of the human experience on earth, and it certainly does not diminish the good that occurs here too. Every aspect of the human experience is necessary in order to learn and grow in all the ways we came here to. Nonetheless, balance is needed. Earth attempts to correct imbalances because the Universe itself functions at perfection. This attempt for equilibrium occurs constantly on all levels from an individual, up to more global issues like the environment. How is balance restored? Karma. If you are hateful in any way to another, eventually, you can expect to experience the same whether in the same form or not. If a company mistreats its employees or is unethical, somehow, they will be held accountable. If you are cruel to another person or take advantage of them, you too can expect the same at some point. You see the trend. In these situations, and situations that are similar, every action has an equal and opposite reaction, like in physics. Balance is restored. In the case of more global issues like the environment, balance is regained by initiating an opposite force. If the environment becomes imbalanced, whether due to people or other factors, the earth will unleash events to attempt to restore balance whether by way of weather, famine, desertification, or other natural means. Until equilibrium is reached, the cycle will continue.

The type of balance I most struggle with is juggling my connection to the spiritual world with my day to day life on earth. When my journey first began and until recently, I found myself almost having an out of body experience for most of the day; it was as if I was not present in my physical body. My head was in the clouds and I was either daydreaming or receiving wisdom from the other realm. It was not healthy for me to live this way because obviously right now I live on earth, and need to be present and living earthly life as well. I needed to find a balance between my two worlds. I have worked on grounding myself in the physical world and focusing more of my attention on being in the present moment here on earth. While the task is not always easy because I am drawn to the spiritual world, I feel more clear and vital when I remain centered and balanced between my two worlds. I share this example with you because many of you may experience this same difficulty when you embark on your journey. As you learn new information and begin to awaken, sometimes another realm feels more like home to you. Even so, you cannot sacrifice your life on earth and the important experiences to be had here to live in an altered state most of the time. The journey is about living life on earth while still having a heightened awareness where you collect lessons that awaken and advance your soul.

To me, balance boils down to being conscious. You must be conscious of your environment so you do not cross the line into imbalance which means you need to monitor your surroundings, ensuring your choices support this state. You must also be conscious of your being, maintaining balance between experiencing the spiritual while living in the physical world. The best way to sustain balance in each case is to listen to your inner voice. You and the Divine know better than anyone what you need. When you listen to this voice and then follow its guidance, you are able to find your balance.

∞ VISUALIZATION AND TIME ∞

Connected

When the stars align, I feel as I

Soar high to meet them.

All my worries fade, as my right way is

Illuminated by the light of the stars.

I follow them along the way, living my life as I may

Leave stardust in my wake.

All is well. All is well.

As I connect and grasp the stars.

They are aligned.

∞VISUALIZATION∞

Most of us have a vision for our life, how we would like to see the future unfold. We visualize our dreams becoming reality, we visualize life going our way, we visualize little things day to day that we believe will bring us joy. Visualizing is an important aspect of the journey. One thing to keep in mind is like attracts like. Whatever energy you project; joy, pain, anger, love, et cetera, is what you will see appear in your life. If you are constantly visualizing yourself receiving fantastic news or reaching your goals, you will attract these events into your life. However, if you consistently visualize something bad happening to you, or believe that nothing will go your way, you will attract these things into your life too. This is why it is crucial to monitor where you focus your energy and be cognizant of your thoughts because they really do create your reality.

I have a process when I consciously visualize something. First, I picture whatever it is I would like to see unfold in my life. I truly put myself in it. I see it, feel it, and act as if it is happening now. Then, I let it go. More simply, dream, ask, act, let go. Release it to the Universe. When you first dream of something or visualize it happening, the first step to make it reality is initiated because the seed is planted. Once you have decided that this is your dream and that you really would like to have it happen or to experience it, ask the Universe to bring it to you. Do not tell the Universe how it must unfold, just ask that it will unfold. When you try to control how every aspect of everything will play out, your dreams and other good experiences have difficulty reaching you because the rigidity blocks the Divine nature of the Universe and the path to reach you. You are better off remaining open to how events play out and find you, and simply focus on the "what" rather than the "how." Once you have asked, you must act as though you already have what you are asking for. This energy alerts the Universe that you are ready to accept, and that the physical world needs to mirror the "visualized" world. Finally, let go. Do not try to force anything, just allow it to be if it is meant to be. I accept the place or situation I am currently in, but continue to believe my visualizations will become reality if they are meant to. These last two steps are perhaps the most important. Letting go is critical because if you hold on to something too tightly, you are incapable of seeing what is in front of you and following the steps before you. You may miss the turn that gets you what you are seeking if you are too consumed by the visualization. Letting go allows that which you seek to find you at the right time. The greatest situations tend to find us when we do not force them, but rather allow them to freely come to us. While you must let go, you must continue to believe. I know this sounds like a contradiction, but it works. When you release your visualizations to the Universe, but continue to believe they are possible, the energy you create in doing so will find you when the timing is perfect. Remember, just because something does not happen right away does not mean it will never happen. We cannot see all of the plan, so we do not know the reasons behind timing. If what you have visualized is destined to be, then it will be. However, not every visualization we have is destined to be, and we have to understand that our life unfolds as it is meant to. I once saw a quote that perfectly describes the journey and visualizing. "You may not end up where you thought you would be, but you always end up where you are meant to be."-Unknown I am actually glad this is the case. There have been times I have visualized something, say a place I thought I wanted to live, or a goal I thought I wanted to achieve, but later realize something better is in store. What if just because I visualized them, they had happened? I would not have been happy like I had thought I would be, but instead, I would be visualizing something different. Similarly, there have been numerous times where my visualizing has been rather murky or fuzzy. I know I want something or I have a general idea, but I cannot decide for sure, so I vacillate. When this happens, you send the Universe mixed signals; in a sense, you ask for two contradictions. How can you live the life of your dreams if you send mixed signals? You cannot have both at the same time, and chances are you would not enjoy that outcome. Competing energy makes it nearly impossible to manifest. As a result, in these instances, I have come to realize it is best to completely let your questioning go and give your power to the Universe. Just ask that the perfect situation or path be given to you, and leave it at that. Sometimes simplicity is the best option. Better to be confident in a generalization than unsure of a specificity. The Universe knows best, and sometimes, those visualizations that do not come to fruition or those that are more general, are actually Divinely sent, and instead something better that we could not have imagined happens. The Universe knows our path better than we do, so why try to fight it? What is meant to be will be.

When manifesting, you may feel as though you are not a part of the material world, as if you are in a different plane with no limitations. From your vantage point, with what you think you know, it seems like the physical world is lagging behind what you feel/think/know will happen. You may think to yourself "It has already happened, the physical world just has to catch up..." In some regards this is true. What you feel and see is happening out there, but it does not automatically mean it will translate down here. Some manifestations are not meant to be experienced by you on earth, but are rather meant to remain a possibility in a different space. An ironic aspect of manifesting is we tend to feel as though we are ahead of the game and are waiting on someone else, or something else to align. As great as this would be, this is not always the case. Oftentimes, we are the physical aspect that the Universe is waiting on to catch up. Sometimes, we are the piece that is yet to fall into place. All of the knowledge, solutions, and answers exist out there, we just have to catch up down here. We must accept what is and plan for the future based on what we presently know. We cannot force our ideal life, what we think we want, into being. We plan for what we know today, but continue to visualize our dreams, knowing that life can change in an instant, and there is much we do not know and cannot perceive. Living in the moment means accepting what is and making the most of it. After all, it is all we are guaranteed. Desperation only creates a block between you and your dreams. It breaks the connection between your manifestations and the Universe because it is a negative quality. If you wish to experience your dreams, be patient; when the time is right, they will find you.

I saved perhaps the most important facet of visualizing for last. Patience. One of the big lessons I am still attempting to master. When you visualize something, or even as you continue along the journey, it is difficult not to become consumed with thoughts about what the future holds and how everything will play out. As humans, we like to have control over our lives, and to know what is coming next so we may prepare. But, we are meant to live in the moment, to enjoy each step along the way. If we are constantly planning for and focusing on the future, we cannot enjoy the present. It is a pattern because we only live in the present moment. There will always be a future to visualize and worry about. We will never be able to escape this, and if we are not conscious in the present moment, we will become consumed by the chase and will never be satisfied. Patience forces us to live in the moment, to take a step back, and to allow life to unfold according to the Divine plan. As difficult as this is, it is necessary if you wish to fully grasp the journey and experience the purity of living in the moment. The present is our current experience that guides the future moments and provides insight into the past. It is an important and necessary reality of the journey.

Living in the present moment can be difficult for many of us, especially if we are unhappy in our present environment. Nonetheless, to receive the most from our journeys, we must live in the present moment; this is where our lives take place, and where all of the growth happens. Living in the moment has been one of my most difficult tasks on the journey, so I devised an exercise that immediately summons your consciousness back to the present when it begins to wander. When I notice myself slipping away back into the past, or into daydreams about the future, I become aware and grounded in the present moment by walking myself through my physical actions at that exact moment. For example, if I am driving in the car, I will say to myself, "I am in _____ city, and

I am driving in the car." I will repeat this to myself a couple of times, and as silly as it may sound, this small action makes it nearly impossible to become lost in anything but the present because it forces your attention back into the moment. It is only when we appreciate the present moment that we can enjoy the rest of the journey.

∞TIME∞

Time is a difficult concept to grasp. It is not physical, nor concrete. "Time" as we understand it is human made. The rest of the Universe experiences time more fluidly as time is not linear, but rather cyclical. The past, present, and future are all connected to one another. In essence, time is a facade. Therefore, everything already exists in some dimension. We experience reality mainly in the third dimension, but there are realities unfolding in each moment in other dimensions that we just cannot perceive. This helps to explain why there is an unlimited number of possibilities for how an event will occur or unfold. Truth and reality lie in the unseen. There is no telling when a possibility will enter into our physical dimension of reality. The implications of this is what allows us to manifest our dreams. It means that our manifestations exist somewhere in the Universe, and we just have not been able to experience them in our time. When we do have these experiences, or a visualization becomes reality, it is because "time" on earth has aligned with "time" in the Universe. This is synchronicity. I call it Divine timing. What I gather from this is anything is possible because it is happening now somewhere, even if we cannot perceive it or live it currently. By visualizing and then relinquishing our control, these possibilities may align in our dimension of reality. It must be noted that time cannot be confined or captured. There is no expiration date for our manifestations and dreams. We also cannot control when each piece aligns because time is fluid and cyclical. We have to remember and remain grounded in the fact that if something is meant to be, it will happen in perfect timing, not our idea of timing. This is key. We can visualize anything we want, but it will only happen if it is right for us, and when the time is right. It is not possible to skip steps and jump ahead; to experience something today that is intended to happen five years from now. This would impede the Divine plan. Our path unfolds in Divine timing, and so we must continue to take the steps laid out before us, living in each moment. Since our time is different from "time" in the Universe, we may feel it takes far too long for something to unfold when in the Universe it happens in the blink of an eye. It could also be that time aligns quickly and it feels like an event unfolds fast. There is no way to predict how time will play out because it cannot be controlled. Just know that our lives and our path unfold how they are meant to in the time they are meant to.

An example of visualizing and time that I recently experienced was the timing of this book. I initially wanted to write it a few years ago. I visualized it being completed, but anytime I began writing it, the words either did not flow or I did not like what I was writing. It was not until recently that I felt compelled to begin again. As soon as I began, the words have flowed much more effortlessly, and all of the pieces are coming together quickly. Clearly in this case my idea of the perfect time was different from the Universe's idea of the perfect time. It was necessary for me to follow the steps as I was being led to take them rather than trying to force them. My feeling is the end result of anything is as perfect as can be when you follow the Universe whereas when you try to force something that is not meant to be, it rarely works.

One final thought on time. We never seem to have enough of it; and there are no guarantees. Nobody knows how much physical time they will be given. While in some ways this thought can be sad, we can also use this to make the most of each moment we are given. To be present, to live our life's purpose, to make a difference, to love one another. Why wait? We must make each moment of time we are given count because each moment is a gift, full of possibilities. Use your moments completely by always remaining aligned to your life path and life's purpose.

∞FEAR∞

In the Depths

In the depths are where the answers
lie, but no matter how hard I try,

The distance consumes me.

Perhaps the key to an epiphany is to let go entirely.

In times such as these, I am reluctant
to see; I allow fear to invade me.

What to expect?

What will I see?

Is the journey safe for me?

But, if I wish to reach the answers
and wisdom that I seek,

I know I must relinquish my control and let go.

And as soon as I am free, all of the answers
and wisdom will be within reach,

And I will experience epiphanies.

In the depths are where the answers
lie, now I know that I

Am able to reach them.

For when I am no longer afraid, I
know a vast journey awaits,

Where I will cover great lengths.

The answers and wisdom will be revealed,

For without fear, nothing is concealed.

∞FEAR∞

Everyone has fears. Whether the fear is of aspects of the journey itself, failure, or a specific event, the effect is the same. Whatever the fear is, when it invades your thoughts, it begins to control your life. You are unable to take steps forward because fear holds you firmly in place. If, however, you can let go of your fears, awakening and fulfilled dreams are within reach. How do you let go of fear? First, understand that fear is a figment of the human mind. You can make a conscious decision not to allow fear to control you or your actions. In the spiritual realm, fear does not exist. There is no need for it. While it is something we all grapple with in the physical world, we do not need to give it the power to ruin our lives. We can overcome our fears because they are not needed, and as a result, we can reach our highest potential. Yes, fear has this big of an impact on your life; the reason being fear is a self-fulfilling prophecy. If you expel a great deal of energy and focus on your fears, they have a way of manifesting into reality. So, what could have remained a potentiality in another dimension, suddenly becomes your physical reality, all because of the energy poured into it. Negativity perpetuates greater negativity, and fear is negative. As a result, fear is not constructive, but is destructive because it has the potential to hold you back. Fear conceals the truth because it clouds your perception. You do not perceive your reality accurately through the lens of fear. It distorts your vision and causes you to feel a sense of negativity towards a scenario or experience that most likely will be perfectly fine or positive. However, you are unable to understand this when your fears get out of hand. You can no longer see the truth. When you have overcome your fears and doubts, your perception is more clear, and the truth can be attained. Choose to work towards letting your fears go. It may not happen overnight, but over time, they will become inconsequential. Take small steps towards letting your fears go. Telling yourself that you have nothing to fear is a start. As you are comfortable, push yourself to take small action steps that correspond to your fear. For example, if you are afraid of failure, ask yourself why you feel this way, and then do something that challenges that fear. Begin to take steps that will lead to your success, do so with a positive attitude, and know that so long as you do your best, you will succeed. My greatest fear used to be the repercussions for letting go. I thought I needed to hold on to dreams, goals, and physical reality to stay in control in order to accomplish what I needed to accomplish and if I let go, I would lose it all. In slowly working towards letting go more frequently, I found I had nothing to fear, and that in fact letting go brought more positivity and abundance to me. You owe it to yourself to try to live a life without fear, where nothing is holding you back. Do not be afraid to venture deeper into the unknown or deeper into yourself. Whatever you encounter along the way, know you can handle it because the Universe never gives you more than you can handle. Your strength may be tested, but you will make it to the other side.

Worry. It is synonymous with fear in terms of its effect on the journey. When you worry, you send out vibrations that contradict what you are really asking for. When you worry, you actually manifest your worries into reality because you expel a great deal of energy towards whatever it is you are focused on. Worry serves no purpose. All it causes is more worry until you have worked yourself up to the point of making your worries reality and being unable to move past them. Worry has the potential to stop you dead in your tracks. It will paralyze you if you allow it to. Worry does not get you to where you wish to be, it does not help you, nor does it advance you. When you overcome doubt, fear, and worry, nothing is holding you back, and you are free to move forward. How do you eradicate worry? Understand that you are bigger than whatever it is you worry about. You are not your worries. Your path is not your worries. They are separate from you, and you have the power to overcome them. Believe you have the tenacity to overcome obstacles positioned on your path. Know that everything you encounter has purpose even if you cannot presently understand it. When you stop worrying and start living in the moment, you see your path as it unfolds directly before you. The steps that matter most are the ones you are taking now. You cannot worry about steps of the past, or the steps you will take in the future because you only have today.

You have more strength than you know, and sometimes you have to be knocked down to your knees to see what you need to see, and then get back up. The key is to remember to get back up again. Sometimes the greatest moment of clarity comes when we are blinded by the darkness or fear because it is then that the light truly shines. When we are so shaken by what is going on around us, we are almost jolted into seeing more clearly, and seeing new and different avenues. The greatest part about when we hit "rock bottom" is we have nothing left to lose. Oftentimes at rock bottom we are able to find our strength, and use it to create positive change. Amid the rubble, we can choose to build our structure back up, or continue to sift through the rubble, and wallow. The best option is to rebuild and rise. When our perspective shifts, and brings us into an awareness where we realize that anything is possible, and no dream is too big because we have nothing left to lose, we must go for it. In these times, stand up, rebuild, and thank the Divine for allowing you to see what it is you desperately needed to see. If we allow the darkness or fear to invade our being, we miss the opportunity to progress and learn. Oftentimes peaks lie just around the corner, and if we allow fear or darkness to petrify us, we cannot reach those peaks. Sure, to reach a peak we must climb, which takes effort, but once the peak is reached, you can never imagine not reaching it. The rewards far outweigh the uphill battle. Along the way, you learn more lessons and accomplish pieces of your mission. In order for the fantastic experiences and opportunities to transpire, we must let go of fear and uncertainty, and allow ourselves to reach farther, having faith that we are on the right track and extraordinary lessons and experiences are within our reach. Any new venture conjures up a certain degree of fear, it is normal. What cannot happen is allowing the fear to hold you back and prevent you from moving forward towards living your life's purpose and accomplishing all you have to accomplish. When you fear the unknown or how the journey will end, transmute the fear into fuel to carry you forward. Make the fear work for you rather than allowing the fear to control you.

You are never alone. Trust that you are always protected by love and light, so there is nothing to fear. You are completely supported every step of the journey by all that is the Universe. Even if you are facing uncertainty or you feel that nobody can understand your situation, you always have the support and protection of a realm governed by love and light. While you may not always see it, you can always feel it. Find confidence in the fact that you are stronger than you realize, and you have the support of the Universe at all times. In moments where fear or desperation gets the best of you, remember that desperation only lowers your vibration and manifests your fears quickly. Take a breath, steady yourself, and repeat a mantra that empowers you to feel confident in your path and the direction you are heading. The mantra can be as simple as "I am supported on my perfect path and I have nothing to fear." Regain control of the present moment so you may eradicate fear and transform your feelings into something more useful; positive change. Remember, sometimes you need to take a risk in order to take flight.

Change

It comes when you are least expecting,

Encouraging you to change course.

The changes lead to an awakening if
you remain open and do not force.

Follow the course set out before
you, signaled by the change,

And you will begin to see all of the opportunities

Embedded in change.

It may come when least expected,
but it opens new doors,

And when you follow through, you
will awaken even more.

∞CHANGE∞

The journey brings with it a lot of change. You will notice changes in yourself as you assimilate new lessons and truths into your being. As a result, you will see your environment change to reflect the new and awakened you. New people will enter your life, while others will leave. Your priorities and interests may shift as well. A new perspective and view will change your reality as you see things you never saw before because you are viewing the world through a different lens. Change helps to get you to where you need to be on the journey. It helps you to advance. If I have learned anything, it is to expect change, and roll with it. It keeps life interesting and helps take you to new and exciting places both within yourself and your experiences. Fighting change will only bring about suffering. You can gain the most from change by accepting it and using it to find opportunities to live your dreams and become more enlightened on the journey.

There is peace within the chaos. Even though at first glance change may seem to bring more chaos than it does peace, if you look deep enough, you are sure to find peace. After all, every storm has calm at its center. There is always something orderly about chaos and change. Usually, they come about during a time when you are straying from your path or losing yourself, or when pieces to the puzzle are ready to come together. It sounds counter-intuitive, but change can ground you. While chaos is typically viewed as making life fall apart, it can just as easily bring life together. Change can allow you to recalibrate and find your center again. It can place you back onto your path by showing you the way. When an event or experience needs to occur to move your life forward, chaos and change appear as well. Some chaos is needed to restructure life, but with this chaos eventually comes peace as all falls into place. It is important to remember that no matter how enlightened you become, you will still experience change, sadness, and challenges in your life. You are never exempt from these experiences. How the journey changes these experiences is the meaning you derive from them, and the attitude you choose to have about them. An enlightened person knows that even the unfavorable moments have purpose and are necessary to move you forward into finer moments. Every moment has purpose.

Change can be perceived as either good or bad, but regardless, all change is meant to be or it would not occur. Whether or not the change is enjoyable is beside the point. Since it is necessary for some reason, perhaps beyond our knowing, it must be accepted. It is simpler to adapt and make the best of any given situation rather than fight it. When you fight, you cause yourself more pain because all of your energy goes to this cause, and the negativity and discord weighs you down. When you accept change for what it is, while remaining open, you become free. Remember, different is not always a bad thing. Change can be good for the soul. New situations and experiences bring with them tremendous opportunity for growth and fulfillment. Without change, new opportunities would not be possible, so in order to have new and exciting opportunities, change is necessary. Without change, growth is not possible. It teaches you. One can learn a lot from experiencing upheavals. They tend to point out your strengths as well as your weaknesses by showing you every side of yourself. You can learn much about yourself based on how well you handle change, and how you allow it to have an impact on you. Do you curl into a ball and spiral downward, or do you rise to the occasion and engage? Since change cannot be controlled, it does not do any good to resist and shut down. It is best to face change head on, do everything you can to navigate it positively, and then rise.

Miracles

*Miracles typically define the awe-inspiring
times when we fold our hands and say*

We are grateful on this day.

*But, what if it was also true that
"bad" times are miracles too?*

*These miracles could be meant to pave the way,
and show us which path we are meant to take.*

*If this is true, then ALL miracles,
both subtle and clear*

*Remind us to have no fear, to trust in
The Plan, have faith, look up,*

And say, everyday,

I am grateful for all of the miracles in my life.

They are gifts of the Highest Power, sent to inspire,

All who encounter them.

∞MIRACLES∞

It is frequently believed that in order for something to be considered a miracle, it must be good, happy, and outwardly positive. However, as humans, we only see so much of what is actually happening all around us. I liken it to an iceberg; you see the tip, but most of it lies beneath the surface where we cannot see it. The same is true of events and times in our lives. We are all guilty of taking them at face value, it seems good, so it must be good, or it makes us feel bad, so it must be bad. In reality, it is not this simple. Sometimes, the "bad" times are actually a positive in our life that we will not understand until a later date. When I was bullied and experiencing what I perceived to be a low point in my life, I did not see until later on that this event was the trigger that launched my spiritual journey which led me to where I am today. If I had not experienced this "bad" event, I do not believe I would be who I am today; a much stronger, wiser, and more enlightened person than before. "Bad" times have purpose too, and can guide us to take a different direction, or to make a different decision. They may also prevent something from happening that would be more detrimental to our life. We do not know what a "worst possible situation" would really look like, or what constitutes rock bottom. It is possible that seemingly bad times are not actually as bad as they appear, and they could lead to a great moment in our life. As cliché as it sounds, everything really does happen for a reason, and everything works out as it is meant to. For those who know this to be true, you cannot pick and choose when this applies. If you believe this when life is good and you are in a great place, then it is also true in trying times as well. You must realize that all of life's events are part of a grand, intricate plan whose blueprints we do not possess. Therefore, we must have faith in the Divine architect and truly believe that while we may not know why something happens to us, even the "bad" happens for a reason and furthers us on our journey. What this all means is the next time you encounter something you perceive as bad, take a step back, and try and see it from a different perspective. Maybe it is setting you up for something better to come along, or perhaps it is pushing you to make a needed change. Everything has purpose. We just have to trust in it.

I have found gratitude to be of tremendous importance in any given situation. It has the power to lift you and to change you and your environment. Being grateful is easy during blissful times, but being grateful during distressing times...? We always think to say thank you or to project loving, happy vibes during times we are happy and life is going our way.

Sometimes even during these times, we may forget to acknowledge it. Few people think to be grateful during dark periods because it seems there is nothing to be grateful for. In my experience, there is always something to be grateful for; something that could have been worse, or something good within the bad no matter how seemingly small. I make an effort to consciously acknowledge my gratitude in life, whether it be during times of great happiness or during times where I am lost. If we shift our perspective and consciousness to gratitude, everything changes. You immediately place yourself into a positive space, and you will then begin to see positive results. The more grateful you are, the more space you hold for gratitude, the more you will find to be grateful for. A beneficial practice that should be a part of everyone's daily routine is to make a list of everything in your life to be grateful for. Your list can range from people, to physical objects, to experiences, to feelings, anything at all. Now whenever you are having a difficult day or you feel like you are stuck in a negative space, you can reference your gratitude lists or make a new one in your mind. You will find your mood and outlook immediately improve as you shift your focus to one of gratitude. There is much to be grateful for, we just need to choose to see it.

Openness

An open heart, and open mind

Allow the greatest opportunities to become aligned.

This openness creates a oneness with the Universe

And you experience bliss.

An open heart and open mind

Help you to remain aligned.

∞OPEN∞

Expectations=limitations. This is something that I had difficulty accepting because I have had expectations my entire life. I am the type of person who would fixate on the future, plan my next step, and develop expectations relating to those steps and to the future. It has taken me a long time to finally realize that expectations create limitations because when we set the bar and lock it into place, we can no longer see alternative paths that may be better suited for us, and we are disappointed when life plays out differently than we had hoped. The reality is life rarely plays out how we expect it will, and the best course of action is to stop creating expectations and to remain open to life, taking each experience in as it comes. Our expectations may cause us to completely miss out on something great or a fabulous opportunity because we were too busy waiting for our expectations to be fulfilled. Our expectations limit our ability to remain open to different opportunities that may be better than anything we ever could have imagined. Without expectations our paths are clear for our lives to unfold perfectly as only a journey without limitations can. As a result, I now remain open to all of life's opportunities where limitations are not in existence, even if it means forgoing building expectations. When we free ourselves from expectations, we are left with openness. This openness is what allows us to experience a path more deep and more rewarding, where we are truly able to enjoy the ride because we are open to whatever comes our way.

Remaining open not only means eliminating our expectations, but also means not giving up on the journey. Yes, there may be frustrating times where it may seem easier to just throw your hands up and stop, but you must continue forward. There is much to see and much to learn; one moment does not define the journey for you. The journey is comprised of countless moments that all culminate in the overall journey. All types of moments are required for a complete journey that results in growth and enlightenment. In other words, we need the favorable times just as much as we need the trying times. We learn from all experiences, and each experience brings us closer to our goals. Remain open to the process and keep going. There is joy and potential with every turn when we are open.

In addition, we must remain open to new ideas. I have found the more open you are, the more creative ideas will find you. Suddenly, that problem you have been having that seems impossible to solve finds the perfect solution. By remaining open to new ideas, you also remain open to learning new lessons and to gaining a greater perspective. It is often after hearing an idea that is foreign to us that we begin to see new connections, learn new lessons, and advance our being to a new level. If you close yourself off to seeing different possibilities, how can you grow as both an individual and spiritual being? You could miss the very things that propel you forward, instead remaining static. When in doubt, seek guidance, again remaining open to the answers. At times, guidance from the Universe does not make sense to us because we do not see the entire picture, and cannot grasp where the path is leading. By remaining open to the answers, guidance may unlock new doors for us. With a more open mind, different experiences have a way of unfolding. You place yourself on a higher level that leads to experiences that match. When open to the journey, you receive the most from it because you allow it to unfold as it should, going wherever it leads you. Being open to the journey does mean that you will experience more highs and lows in greater depth, but this only makes the journey more exciting, interesting, and inspiring. Keep your eyes open, keep your mind open, go where the journey leads you, even if the territory is uncharted. In the end, the guidance you receive, and the experiences you encounter will be all the reassurance you require to remain open. The journey is impressive for those who take the leap.

∞LET GO∞

Let Go

Let go of the pain and suffering of the past,

Let go of the hardships and toxic relationships

Holding you back.

Let go of negativity, frustration, and lack.

For once you let go, they can no longer take hold.

You are free to move forward,

And without excess weight,

The limits are untold.

∞ LET GO ∞

Letting go is pivotal to awakening and walking along the enlightened path. If you wish to move forward, you must first let go of past negativity. The weight will hold you back and prevent you from evolving and progressing. There is no purpose to holding on to past negative experiences or emotions; the past is in the past, and playing them on loop only traps you and keeps you stuck in that general pattern of pain. You cannot lament or be fearful that history will repeat itself. Life is meant to be lived. There is purpose in those painful experiences when they happen because they provide a prodigious environment for growth and learning, but when relived, they create a rut. Let go of negativity. There is something very freeing when you are finally able to let go of all that is negative in your life. New opportunities, people, and lessons present themselves because there is room for them. Take the lessons you were meant to learn from an experience with you, move forward with a heightened awareness. Be grateful for where you are today and the lessons the past taught you.

Often, we are afraid to let go, but what we fail to realize is holding on can hurt us more. Imagine you are poised, ready to take a leap leading to your dreams. In one scenario, you are attached to a bungee cord (symbolizing all you are holding on to) that is too short, and in the other, you are attached to nothing. In the bungee cord scenario, you jump, but instead of flying, you retract because the cord is too short, causing you to be left dangling mid-air, stuck. But, in the scenario where you are not attached to anything, you jump and fly. You experience less pain and more joy with nothing weighing you down. Holding on will hold you back, but letting go will set you free.

Letting go is like cutting down a tree. If the tree has a disease, it will continue to spread unless you remove its roots. Once the roots are dug up, the disease can no longer spread to other trees. The same is true of experiences, negativity, and events. If you view everything you are holding on to as trees whose roots are all connected, then you can see what happens by holding on to negative emotions, events, and experiences. They spread via their deep roots and begin to infect all of the positive, healthy trees until all you have left is negativity as well as toxicity. However, if you are able to let go of the unhealthy, negative "trees," over time, the positive "trees" become abundant and begin to change your perception and subsequent reality.

You cannot truly begin to move forward until you have let go of that which does not serve you. Good or bad, you cannot hold on to a moment or fragment of time. When you attempt to hold on, <u>it</u> holds you back by capturing your being and your awareness so you are frozen in that space. By remaining frozen, you fail to see your reality and all the possibilities and future moments to be had. Each moment moves us forward and brings us closer to the truth and to our destiny, but only when we free ourselves to experience them, one at a time. How do you know of what to let go? Any negativity whether in the form of feelings, fears, or experiences must be rectified. Beliefs or ideals that force you to attempt to attain something that is not meant for you must be let go so your path becomes clear. Relationships that have served their purpose or are holding you back must be let go so you may grow and move forward. Essentially anything that you are harboring that makes you feel distressed or stuck on the inside must be released for your greater good. As soon as you are able to let go, the path clears, and new doors open. Better situations, people, and opportunities find you as soon as you let go. This is because your perfection is able to reach you when you create the space to receive it.

This is one of the more difficult lessons and actions, to let go, but it is associated with every other lesson on the path. You cannot fully grasp all there is to know until you can let go. A quote from Lao Tzu sums it up perfectly, "Life is a series of natural and spontaneous changes. Don't resist them; that only creates sorrow. Let reality be reality. Let things flow naturally forward in whatever way they like." When you live in the moment and let go of the past as well as the unknowns of the future, you can find happiness and peace in just allowing and going with the flow of life. Once you let go, you can then move forward and old patterns or wounds can longer hold you back. Letting go sets you free.

∞ H E A L ∞

A large part of the journey relates to not only letting go but also to healing. The two are inextricably linked. First, you must let go, as mentioned earlier, but then you must heal. Part of the process of awakening is healing old patterns of thinking, old wounds, or old pieces of yourself that must evolve. After a difficult time in your life, or even as you learn new truths and lessons, it is imperative that you allow yourself time to heal in order to move forward. If we do not heal, these pieces of the past will continue to have a firm grip on our future by perpetuating the pain and negativity. Only by letting go of them and healing the space may we escape this detrimental cycle.

Healing takes time. So long as you are making an effort to heal, you will begin to see results. Healing works most effectively and efficiently when you allow yourself to feel what you are feeling in the moment. Let it out. You are human, and you have the right to feel whatever it is you are feeling. It is actually worse to stifle your emotions than to feel them briefly and then move on. Until we resolve conflict or emotion, it finds ways to be expressed even if outwardly we appear to be fine. Feel it, scream, cry, however you need to find peace, but, once you have let it out, let it go. The longer you hold on to pain and suffering, the more difficult it is to move past it and heal. You begin to heal as you put the experience or emotion behind you and realize that through letting go and healing, you move forward with greater clarity. Eventually, you reach a point when old triggers no longer generate a reaction from you. It is also possible to find the need to heal an issue that you did not realize was an issue for you on the surface. I have worked with individuals who thought they were neutral when it came to past experiences, but in further talking, realized these experiences still held a great deal of emotion that was negatively affecting them. As soon as these realizations were had, they could heal these wounds they thought were gone. Only when you become aware, can you allow healing to begin.

Not only must we heal on an emotional, spiritual level, but we must also at times heal on a physical and energetic level. After a battle with illness, disease, trauma, an accident, or physically grueling time, we must allow ourselves to heal physically and energetically. Why? There is an undeniable connection between the mind and the body, or as I prefer to view it, energy and the body. When we can heal from physical afflictions, we also begin to mend energetic problems, and vice versa.

A very personal example of healing physically, emotionally, and energetically is when I was experiencing severe stomach issues stemming from allergies, and the pain from the difficult period in my life due to being bullied. I simultaneously worked through each, changing my diet to be free of the allergens and also more healthful while also researching how to make my body strong again. I began to let go of the bullying experience by turning it into a positive and helping other victims of bullying through public speaking and the creation of a booklet. As I continued to focus on moving forward and letting go of the past, understanding that these hardships no longer served me, I began to heal. The process took time, but with each stride I could feel my energy shift into a more positive and light state which in turn helped me to physically feel better, and to emotionally be able to focus on all that was good and positive instead of the negativity of the past.

Beyond the Bounds

Beyond the bounds of bodies

*There is a space where free form reigns and
energy dances to a different vibration.*

*Here, you are free to be, anything;
everything you yearn to be.*

Beyond the bounds of bodies

Lies a space past earthly eyes,

*Where souls explore something
more and awaken to ALL.*

Back in the bounds of bodies

With all of the constraints,

The space becomes a distant dream,

Unless you profess that <u>you are</u> free to be.

*When the limits are removed, the
space envelopes you into an*

Endless embrace.

∞PERSPECTIVE∞

Perspective has the ability to shape our experiences as well as determine how deeply we understand them. When you think about it, most of us have encountered experiences where viewing them one way, they seem upsetting, but if viewed a different way, from a different perspective, they were actually quite Divine. This is the power of perspective. When changed, our views, and as a result, our world, is changed too. Perspective has the power to either elevate us or sabotage us, and the view we choose to take is the deciding factor. We control our perspective and subsequent experience through our attitude. A negative individual will be perpetually stuck in whatever quagmire they find themselves in because their perspective, which is most likely narrow-minded, will prevent them from seeing the solution. Their negativity will keep them down. If this individual shifted their attitude to a more positive one, their perspective would shift, and solutions would become apparent. They would no longer be stuck, and their consciousness would shift to a higher level as well. In essence, if you wish to be happy and enlightened, choose to see the good in every experience. Even if on the surface, something or someone seems bad, try adjusting your perspective, and you will most likely find something good. If you feel that bad things always seem to have a way of finding you, try to become consciously aware of your dominant perspective. More often than not, you probably look for the negative first, so this is all you can see. If you train yourself to pause before judging, and to look at how an experience may be beneficial, you will begin to see the opportunity and lessons embedded in each moment and experience.

For practical purposes, I often view perspective one of two ways. Some situations require you to take a step back, to zoom out in a sense, and to look at the big picture. Other situations require you to take a closer look, to zoom in, and to see how a lesson or experience serves you now. Simply choosing one over the other not only alters your view, but has the potential to change your experience. As an exercise, take a past experience and view it each way. What do you glean from it from a big picture perspective? What role does it play? How does it change your thoughts when dissected and applied to only the time period it occurred in? This exercise will help you to get in the habit of shifting your perspective to get the most from an experience. A lot of times, we do not know of the magnitude or trivial nature of an experience until we become aware of our perspective. You have grasped perspective when you are able to discern which approach to take in each situation.

Perspective and attitude are closely connected. For example, if you typically adopt a positive attitude towards life, your perspective is most likely going to be similar. If you are more negative and woeful, your perspective will probably match. Therefore, if you change your attitude, your perspective changes over time as well. You position yourself to see each situation for what it offers you, and to see the good in all of it. Being more positive will give you a more optimistic outlook. There is a saying, change your attitude, change your life. The connection between perspective and attitude is part of why this is true. When you change your attitude, this changes your perspective, which in turn changes your life. You have the power to create your experiences through the perspective you choose to take. If you would like to have more positive experiences, then change your attitude and perspective to see the positive things in your life now. This will make the present time more convivial and it will allow the future to be the same.

Ego

The ego is earthly,

A fact of life.

The purpose is to attempt to rise.

Inhabit a space where ego cannot thrive.

When ego is overcome,

You have arrived.

∞ E G O ∞

The ego disconnects us from our authentic being, and impedes our ability to connect to the Universe. This is because the ego is earthly and physical, not etheric and spiritual. Not only is the ego an earthly manifestation, but it is toxic, and therefore lowers one's vibration when activated. When you lower your vibration, you cannot see clearly, you cannot fully understand lessons and the journey, and you cannot move forward to a higher level because the ego has you chained down. When you lower your vibration, the entire planet's vibration is lowered. The good news is when you remove the ego, and raise your vibration, the planet's vibration is raised as well. Energy is fluid, not static, so it is easily changed. When your ego rules your being, it distorts your perception and causes you to focus on and be motivated by the material aspect of things. You are only able to focus on "I" and "Me" rather than "Us" and "We." Whatever it is at the moment that is egotistically driven causes you to become consumed by your ego at the expense of people, perspective, and other aspects of your life. As part of the journey, you come to realize that the journey is larger than yourself; it affects everyone and everything. Instead of supporting and uplifting yourself and others, the ego divides. It divides you into two entities, the physical and the spiritual, and it creates a divide between you and everyone else. When you operate from a divided self, you cannot awaken and fully grasp all there is to know. The physical entity with its ego will drown out any wisdom you may receive from your spiritual self. It cannot be assimilated properly when your physical self is out of tune as it is with ego. You must operate as a whole being, with the physical and spiritual aligned. In order to do this, ego cannot be present. When the two selves are aligned, you may once again be able to incorporate new wisdom and lessons into your entire being. One example of an egotistical mindset that creates division is making assumptions. Most of us are guilty of making assumptions at some point, we do not give someone a chance because we assume we know who they are based on how they present themselves, or we assume that we see the entire picture of events, people, ourselves, and life in general. The list goes on. When we make these assumptions, we diminish whatever it is the assumption is based on, and in turn, we diminish ourselves because we lower our frequency and block growth and enlightenment. Our assumptions are oftentimes false, and we potentially miss out on befriending a wonderful person, exploring an incredible opportunity, or receiving wisdom. This is why we must try to operate without ego; when we do, it sets us back on our journey.

Ego's frequency lowers your vibration and makes it more difficult for you to receive the guidance and lessons that will help you to awaken. When this happens, you begin to stray from the path and allow your ego to guide you. The problem here is your ego has a lust for attention and power, and the more you feed it, the more it craves. If you do not keep your ego in check, it will eventually overpower you, stifling your soul. When your ego is activated, you lose sight of what truly matters, the journey, the lessons, the awakening. It causes you to become consumed by more shallow, physical manifestations that will not add anything to your life in any way, but will actually detract from it. The experiences you yearn for from an egotistical place will not help you to awaken into a higher state of being. Instead, these experiences would place you into a slumber that can only bring suffering. When you shut the ego off, you have the clarity to seek experiences and opportunities that lead to greater growth and fulfillment where deep-seated joy awaits. You can remove the ego a couple of ways. First, you must consciously decide that you no longer wish to feed your ego. This step ensures you remain aware of your ego so you may keep it at bay. As you make decisions throughout the day, stop and ask yourself what is motivating them. Is it ego or is it for the right reasons? Next, you can focus on gratitude, others, and remaining grounded. When you focus on what you are grateful for, your energy shifts into a higher and more deeply connected space. Focusing on others is an excellent way to shift your perspective away from yourself, so you may be of assistance to someone else, and in turn be filled with thoughts of connection and unity rather than separateness which the ego thrives on. Finally, remaining grounded shuts the ego off by reminding you of your place in the world and helps to maintain a clear mind. With thoughtfulness and clarity, the ego struggles to survive. When overcome, you are free to rise and to awaken into your destined self.

∞PEOPLE∞

Infinitely United

United peoples with colorful souls

Connect and know beyond the limits imposed.

As one, go billions, together into infinity.

Colors reflected beautifully.

∞ P E O P L E ∞

As you learn tremendous lessons on the journey and uncover universal truths, you may find other people play a sizable role in your ability to put these lessons and truths into action. Some people will support these lessons, making it easier for you to assimilate them into your life, while others will challenge you and make it more difficult to put these lessons into practice. This is because there is one pivotal lesson that is tied to many others; tolerance. When you think about it, our response to others says a lot about who we are and where we are on the journey. If you claim to have love and respect for everyone, or that you only send out positive vibes, but then you treat others poorly or separate yourself from everyone else, are you really the great things you think you are? Your level of tolerance can illustrate how well you understand the journey. Tolerance works in conjunction with many of the other lessons because it is through tolerance you connect with others. It is through tolerance that you gain perspective into your own life. It is through tolerance that you begin to grasp we are all beings of Light from the same spark, and that we are one. Tolerance means accepting people for who they are, and having respect for perceived differences. Just because you do not understand someone else, their beliefs, or their life, does not mean you are right and they are wrong, or you are better and they are worse. We are just different, and those differences make life beautiful. With tolerance, we allow everyone to be who they are without shame, and continue to support one another while advancing on the journey.

Along with tolerance comes judgement. Do not judge others, we are taught from a young age. This is so simple, yet so difficult to put into action each moment of the day it seems. We have a natural tendency to make judgements against people who are different from us, but what we often fail to realize is everyone has a story. The outer shell that we see on a daily basis is only one very fine layer. As the layers are peeled back, we see who they truly are, and understand there is more than meets the eye. Very seldom are people who they actually appear to be on the surface. More often than not, you must look beneath the surface to uncover who a person is at their core. We see people in one environment, a lot of times only receiving a snapshot of who they are. It is possible that this snapshot occurs in a time in their life where they are struggling with something we know nothing about, or we catch them on a bad day. If we judge them too soon, we not only misunderstand them, but also miss the opportunity to potentially make a connection. People, ourselves included, deserve a chance for their authentic selves to show which can take time. When we pass judgement too quickly we rob that individual of this opportunity, and close ourselves to the truth. By accepting everyone, even our differences, we no longer operate from a place of judgement, but rather one of oneness and Light. The best experiences and opportunities in life come from this dimension of oneness and Light. If we operate from this dimension, our journey will align here too, and this higher vibration will bring with it a more positive experience.

Be an example for others by exemplifying what you wish to see more of in the world. If you want to experience greater compassion, be more compassionate yourself. If you want to raise the global energy level, keep your energy positive. Your thoughts and actions will subconsciously trigger others to behave similarly because the vibrations you send out are magnified and multiplied. Everything and everyone are all connected and we need to rise above the darkness in the world in order to enter into a new age of light. If you rise above and demonstrate love, light, and all things positive, others will follow, and we will see significant changes. One way to foster these changes is to share your journey, and ignite change in others. Having the support of a few key people along the way makes all the difference. Everyone needs someone to support them, someone to share the experiences and lessons with. It is important to invite people into your life who not only support you, but who will help you to grow, allowing you to do the same. Relationships should be balanced. It is necessary to have an equal exchange of energy or you will experience imbalance which leads to toxicity. You cannot be the only one to give, nor can you be the only one to receive. For me, the easiest way to ensure balance is to focus on love and light. This is a way of saying project positivity to others, and find those who do the same for you. Connections that are based on similar experiences and mutual respect will have the most profound impact.

We are all infinite spiritual beings living in a temporary plane. We need one another to collectively advance on a more global journey. It is important to find people with whom you are able to relate, and who you are able to learn from. Without these individuals, the journey would be more difficult and lonely. While you always have the support and encouragement from above, it is nice to have the support and encouragement of others who are on the journey here as well. People have the potential to help mold your experiences and to help you continue the journey. Choose wisely. While the right individuals will enrich the journey, toxic individuals will hinder the journey. If you wish to move forward and experience greater positivity, it is best to let go of toxic relationships in your life now, and prevent toxic relationships from forming in the future. Choose to surround yourself with those who support and encourage you, and who leave a positive mark on your life. Allow them to walk alongside you. These people may not come often, but when they enter our lives, it is for a Divine purpose.

Fractals

As fractals, we are one,

Equals in the whole.

We share a connection

That is both beautiful and bold.

Together we create

An image so Divine,

It has and will continue

To withstand the test of time.

∞CONNECT∞

Everyone and everything is energy, pieces of one consciousness. This means that we are not separate from one another, but rather are fractals in one Divine consciousness. While we may look and act different on the physical plane, our souls belong to a collective consciousness that has and will always be united. We are ONE. Every single person has three attributes in common: a spirit, a soul, and a physical body. Our spirits act as an intermediary between our souls and our physical bodies. The spirit connects the two and acts as our spiritual body, our essence or personality in spiritual terms. The soul holds the wisdom, memories, and knowledge you have accumulated over time and from Home in the spiritual realm. The soul is also our spiritual signature given to us from the Divine whose fingerprint remains with us always. Both the soul and spirit are housed in our physical bodies which act as a vessel for growth, learning, and service in this lifetime. We are equals in these terms as we are all souls here to learn and grow, all with the capacity to reach our full potential. We are all given these three components to begin. Yes, our gifts and abilities may be different, but we are all pieces of the same whole, and should treat one another as such. Our uniqueness is a result of our individual journeys over time that shape us into who we are, and while our connection to one another may at times become strained, it cannot ever be broken because we are one.

We find ourselves in a paradox of sorts because our world is more technically connected now than ever, yet it seems people are more distant than ever before. How is it that during a time when we should be more connected, we are less? Personally, I believe this is because there is little meaning left in the relationships via the technical connections. As pieces of one consciousness, we are built to have the capacity and desire to connect with one another on a deep level, as individuals on a collective journey. We crave meaningful connection, and meaningful connection is missing from many modern forms of connecting, like the internet, social media, or texting. In order to be fulfilled in this sense, and to connect with others, we must create meaning once again which means building relationships in the physical world in addition to the virtual world. Just as technology enables the world to connect via networks and webs, a higher consciousness enables people to connect who share a similar frequency which creates a network as well. Part of the journey is to find people you connect with and to create a network where you share your ideas and experiences and help one another along the way. We form a connection to another when we share our own stories, experiences, and lessons from our journey. A connection is also formed when we offer to help others on their journey however we are able.

The journey is awfully lonely when we choose to walk alone, forgoing any connections. It is more meaningful to establish connections with like-minded spirits who can offer advice as well as an ear to your experiences, feelings, and gifts discovered as you awaken. I know when I first began awakening, I needed a support system and people to share my experiences with. As you open and awaken, it helps to have others who either have experienced or are experiencing the same to share stories with. Having a small group of friends and family who I could trust to open up to, and who could help guide me along the path, has made all the difference in my ability to fully embrace the journey and the process of awakening. You can help and encourage one another to remain true to your path, and to allow your awakening to unfold however it is destined to. I remember the first time I met people who were also on their journey to awakening; it was at a spiritual retreat, and it was the first time since embarking on the journey I could be completely open about my experiences (with someone other than immediate family) because they understood. We shared stories about how the journey began, and what we had discovered about ourselves and what it all meant. They believed in me, and I believed in them. Finding people who can relate to you and support you is not always an easy task, but when you place yourself in situations where there are likely to be others like you, you find you are not alone, and you walk away with new friends, a fresh perspective, and gratitude for not only the journey but also the camaraderie. Some excellent places to find similar individuals are at spiritual retreats, workshops, events, or centers. Many exist, and a quick search can reveal the best and closest option for you. There is a widespread awakening taking place, and as previously mentioned there are a number of opportunities to meet others who are having similar experiences; be open to finding them and allowing them to share in the journey. My closest friends have come into my life since beginning my journey, and I am forever grateful for their friendship and support.

∞GIFTS∞

The Gifts

The gifts rest within,

Different for all.

Our personal mission is to discover them all.

Use our uniqueness, set our gifts free.

Ignite the change that we wish to see.

As we share our gifts

It all becomes clear,

There is power within all,

A magic to be revered.

∞ GIFTS ∞

As many atoms as there are in the Universe, that is how many individual gifts exist within people. It is not possible to articulate each and every gift someone may be blessed with. We are each unique, even though we all originate from the same spark of Divinity, we all have our own gifts. One combination is not better than another; they are just different. Our gifts help us to fulfill our purpose. As with other things in life, some people have many gifts, others have few. Some are powerful and huge, others subtle yet mighty. It is up to us to discover the gifts that rest inside, and as we are guided down our path, new gifts will be uncovered.

What is meant by gifts? I refer to gifts as any ability you excel at, or that is innate. I also believe a gift may be an attribute such as compassion or patience. Lessons may become gifts as well. For me, the lessons make the journey, and I have already learned a great deal. I consider each lesson learned along the way to be a gift because they helped to shape me into who I am today, ultimately leading to increased understanding and awareness. When we learn something new, or master a quality like patience, this is a gift in itself because we now have something of significance that we did not possess before.

The gifts are already within you, from the moment you are born. As the journey unfolds with time, they will be revealed and will come to the surface. There is no maximum number of gifts one may be blessed with. Gifts will continue to be uncovered throughout your journey on earth. In fact, it is part of our mission while on the journey to discover the many gifts we possess. Part of the fun of embarking on your journey is learning about yourself on a deeper level and discovering you have gifts you never realized you had. With these gifts, you can choose if you want to use them and in what capacity. Not every gift is meant to be turned into a career; sometimes we are just meant to use these gifts for ourselves or to gain insight into our own life. You may decide you are not ready to accept the gift, and reserve it for a later time. The choice is yours.

There are gifts I was given that I have chosen not to use, while others are a part of my everyday life. One gift that was revealed to me towards the beginning of my journey was the ability to "see" energy. By this I mean I can see what others may be able to sense. This is sometimes in the form of an illness, energy blockage, negativity, positivity, and the Universe. I am also able to clear negative energy and replace it with positive energy. Another gift is my ability to receive or channel wisdom from the Universe. It is difficult to describe, but it flows through me; sometimes it is intended just to help me, while other times, it is a message that must be shared with others. For example, many of the universal truths I have received on the journey have come to me in this form. I also began to be able to "see" into situations, people, the past, present, and future to access information that could bring forth clarity and healing. I know there are people who either do not believe these are gifts, or who do not believe in them at all. Everyone is entitled to their individual beliefs, but I choose to ignore the voices who are unkind and only listen to those who support me because I know my abilities to be true. You may encounter the same reactions if you choose to reveal some of your own gifts. Do not let those who do not support you keep you from using the gifts bestowed upon you from a Divine power. There will always be those who are unsupportive, but it is your choice whether you listen to them. I encourage you to continue to embrace your gifts and use them however you are guided to use them, whether to help others or just for yourself.

All of your gifts are within reach. While we will use some of our gifts each day, others will only be activated when we choose to use them. For these gifts, it is relatively easy to forget we possess them because they are not being used on a daily basis. I have found it is helpful to use a journal to record new gifts you uncover within yourself because the journal cannot only act as a reminder for you but also as encouragement for when you need extra support. Due to the number of gifts we possess, in many cases, we take them for granted. Some gifts that have always been present at the surface do not register as being special to us because it is normal for us. A few examples of this could be intuition, taking on the emotions of others around you, or having an incredibly accurate read on people. However, if you took on the perspective of someone else, you would see that even some of the "normal" behaviors and attributes we discount are in fact gifts in disguise. We do not always realize our gifts are special or out of the ordinary until we open ourselves up and share with other people. For example, a number of my abilities were innate in me, and looking back, I possessed them at a young age before I was aware of what they all meant. This did not come to light until I began my spiritual journey and spoke to family members and others because these gifts were normal life for me; I had no idea everyone else was not experiencing what I was experiencing. This is why it is a beneficial exercise to occasionally reflect on your most seemingly normal and insignificant attributes because you may find that they are actually some of your greatest gifts that set you apart and aid you on your journey. What you view as normal may very well be unique to you. As you learn more about yourself and your gifts, you are better able to navigate your path in life because you are aware of your strengths and can use them. Another way you may discover a gift is when it is as if a switch was flipped because one day it seems you were without a gift, and the next, it suddenly appears. Sometimes a gift lies dormant until we reach a certain point on the journey, at which point the gift is unlocked. We are not always ready for a gift and all it entails; sometimes it takes additional growth and knowledge before we are ready to accept it. This is all part of the journey; uncovering new gifts we never knew we had and determining how or if to use it. Whether a gift is meant to come into our lives for us to benefit from personally, or to be shared with others is irrelevant in the sense that either way, our gifts should be celebrated because they are gifts, after all... Blessings in disguise. They can help to shape our path depending upon how we use them.

It can be challenging when you discover new gifts you never knew you possessed because depending on what they are, they can bring with them anxiety and uncertainty. Typically you do not see these words associated with the word gift, but in the case of spirituality and awakening, the emotions may be mixed. With some gifts comes a great deal of responsibility, such as when they involve helping or guiding others. Anxiety may become present when you are unsure how to handle or use a gift. I personally experienced a lot of anxiety because first I had to accept my gifts, and then I needed to be led as to how to use them, whether to share them or keep them to myself. At first, I kept them to myself for fear of ridicule and fear of the responsibility attached to them, but as the journey continued, and my gifts became stronger, I knew I needed to share them. This brings us to the uncertainty portion of gifts... While I was unsure how I needed to share my gifts at first, I knew no matter what, my life would change dramatically as a result. The truth is, my life changed dramatically as soon as I discovered my gifts, and what I realized was sharing my gifts and experiences with others would not detract from them, but rather would complement them by allowing me to make a difference. Even though I faced challenges as a result of my gifts, I have also enjoyed prodigious growth, connection, and fulfillment from discovering my gifts as well. Now I am to the point where I would not trade my gifts for anything. I encourage you to come to accept and treasure your own gifts as well as you discover the potential and magic you too possess.

∞FULFILL∞

Fulfill

Fulfill your mission, your reason to be.

Fulfill your hopes and your dreams.

This is the key to feel at peace.

*Whether consciously aware or
uncertain it may seem.*

*When the time comes, you will see
all you are destined to be.*

Be open to your mission, be guided by your dreams.

By doing so you will fulfill your destiny.

∞FULFILL∞

Everyone has a purpose, a reason for being on earth. It may be personal like mastering a skill or learning a lesson or lessons important to your growth. It could be more global like helping other people in some way, or impacting the world on a larger scale with your unique gifts. It could be both. Your purpose is unique just as your journey is unique. It is our job while on earth to not only remember our reason for being, but to attempt to fulfill that reason for being. Some people were born with the ability to remember their purpose; they are the ones who from a young age never waiver on what they would like to do when they "grow up." Others uncover their mission later in life, maybe after searching for happiness in different areas. You may struggle to remember your purpose at any age, or one day it may come to you in a flash. One way to tell if you have already discovered your purpose is to look at your passions. Typically, whatever you are passionate about ties in to your purpose in life. Your unique gifts and abilities also aid you in fulfilling your purpose by providing you with the tools you will need to live your life's purpose.

My purpose actually came to me as I began to awaken and follow my journey. Before this point I was thinking about a career related to science or medicine, but the more spiritual truths, lessons, and pieces of myself I uncovered, the more clarity I received. The path I was meant to follow, and the mission I was destined to undertake was not in either of these fields (while I am still interested in both science and medicine, both assimilate into spirituality for me and are not independent studies). My path was one of spirituality and enlightenment. All I knew at first was that I needed to record all I learned so that at some point, I could share the knowledge I gained with others in an effort to help them on their journey to awakening. Even now, I do not have all of the pieces, nor do I know how everything fits together in terms of my journey and purpose, but this is okay. The journey has more than one stop and objective, and I know when the time is right, everything I need to know will be revealed to me, just as it will be for you. You may not be given all the details or a map with specific steps to fulfill your purpose in advance, but this does not mean you have no purpose. Instead, you must take the journey one step at a time and let it unfold as it will. Your purpose will become clear and you will fulfill it when the time is right for you.

I used to think it was a problem that I wanted to travel down a path different from most, or that what I felt I was meant to do was not enough. After all, there are so many voices out there that try to tell you to do something different or to be something different. "You should get a normal job..." or "You should want to have the same experiences as everyone else your age..." A lot of people are more comfortable with boxes and norms even though many are limiting. They are familiar and expected, therefore they must be correct. I, like many others I imagine, feel that I do not fit, nor am I meant to fit into a traditional mold, and finally, after many lessons, and experiences, I have learned to embrace my uniqueness, and so should you. We did not come to earth to be the same, we came to fulfill our own purpose, in our own way. Molds are meant to be broken. Forge your own path. Live the life you came here to live, and do not listen to those who do not support you. If you have a dream inside of you, let it out. Just because others are not doing the same does not mean you should hold yourself back, or stifle your uniqueness. Someone has to be the first to try something different. Why not you? Trust in yourself. Live life your way not their way. So long as you are happy and feel you are following your path, you have nothing to apologize for.

Only <u>you</u> are able to fulfill your purpose. No matter how long it may take you to discover, it is yours and yours alone. No two people have exactly the same purpose. You may be on a parallel path with another, both working towards a greater good, but everyone has their own unique journey and purpose they must fulfill in this lifetime. There are people you are meant to have in your life who will help you on your journey to fulfilling your purpose, just as you will help others. In the end, only you will accomplish what you need to accomplish, and they will do the same.

We fulfill our journeys bit by bit. It is through small, manageable steps that we complete our missions. It is not possible to take one step and reach the finish line because there are necessary stopping points along the way that are equally as important as the end result. As much as we would sometimes like to blink and reach the destination, it is the entire journey, every step, that makes a lifetime whole and a journey complete. Each step you take towards your destination is something to be celebrated since it is with each step we get closer to the finish line.

Your mission cannot be rushed. It must unfold as it is intended to unfold. Timing really is everything. You have to be ready to fulfill it, and the world must be ready to accept it. It takes time for the two to become aligned. There have been countless times I have felt compelled to take bold action in terms of my mission, but something has stopped me each time. In the moment, it is frustrating because I feel ready, but something just does not click. Soon after, I realize that there was another piece to the puzzle I needed to receive, or a good reason the timing was not quite right yet. You just have to trust in the plan and in your mission, carry on, and know that when the timing is right, all of the pieces will fall into place.

When you know your purpose, take action steps to fulfill it. It does not matter how small, so long as you are working towards the greater goal. You may experience that voice in your head telling you you are not capable or good enough which causes you to procrastinate and put off your mission. That voice is wrong. You are capable. You are good enough. You are worthy. Silence that voice, and choose a mantra that empowers you to keep going. Follow the steps you are guided to take, even if they seem to be baby steps because eventually you will have covered a prodigious distance, and your end goal will be in sight. Nothing compares to the deep sense of fulfillment you experience when you are living your life's purpose.

∞AUTHENTICITY∞

Authenticity is a major lesson and step on the journey to awakening. As you continue to open yourself to the lessons and experiences that accompany the journey, you will find you have less tolerance for inauthenticity or "fake" people. This includes yourself. When you discover new pieces of yourself, or apply new lessons to your life, you will feel a pull to live as authentically as possible. You realize that you have to live your life for you, and do what makes you happy. Living the life you think will bring you happiness, or being the kind of person you think people want you to be will only bring you pain because you are being someone or something you are not. When you make the decision to live an authentic life, being yourself completely and doing what brings you joy, you will be energized and experience pure happiness. Another facet of living authentically is the people you attach yourself to. If you are kind and centered, for example, but you surround yourself with people who are unkind and toxic, you are not living authentically. You must choose to surround yourself with people who allow you to be your most authentic self, and who are also their most authentic selves. The connection is stronger and deeper when authenticity is at the core.

Sometimes what is expected has to be amended to reflect the image of the soul. Inauthenticity is like walking on hot coals; you only get burned. Authenticity, however, lights a fire within that powers you to no end. It is necessary at certain points in our life to take a good look at our lives and focus on how our current path makes us feel. If you find that your current path makes you anxious, nauseous, or unhappy, you probably need to make some changes to be more authentic. These feelings are indicators that you may not be entirely aligned with your purpose, or your authentic self. If you try to force a square peg into a round hole things will not come together; at least not the right things. Something may happen, but not the somethings that would bring you joy. Only authenticity can bring you joy, and if you are being authentic, you will feel energized and at peace; an inner knowing will radiate from your core. Another sign of your level of authenticity is momentum of opportunities. When you have a number of opportunities presented that are all similar to one another or come one right after another, it can indicate that you are on the right track. If you find no opportunities have been presented even with your effort, then it may be time to take a closer look at your actions to ensure you are being your most authentic self. If you find you are chasing a dream that is not yours, release it, and find what will allow you to be <u>your</u> most authentic self.

At times, it can be difficult to be authentic. We fear rejection, judgment, or failure. As unnerving as these possibilities may be, the repercussions of inauthenticity are far worse. If you try to be authentic, you will feel so much better because you are aligned to a far higher power. With authenticity it is important to remember that you always have a choice and free will. If a decision or direction does not feel right or authentic to you, choose to turn a different way that does feel right and is authentic. It can be difficult when other voices try to tell you to go one way, but your heart is telling you something different. Remember that while they have voices, you have a voice as well. You have the power to choose which voice you listen to, and you must use your voice in your quest for authenticity. Choose happiness. Choose passion. Choose to be authentic. Once in this space, you reach the point where it no longer matters what others think, so long as you know what you are doing is right. If you never allow yourself the space to be authentic, and remain in a perpetual state of inauthenticity, the facade will not only wear you down, but it will bar you from living your dreams and fulfilling your purpose. The fears that accompany being authentic are only temporary. The consequences for being inauthentic will last a lifetime.

∞LIVE∞

Create

Creativity is innate.

It rests quietly within;

Until inspiration stirs

And ignites a fire signaling us to begin.

To create. To explore. To transform
the inspiration into more.

This is creativity;

Awakened and realized.

Another Divine reflection bore.

∞CREATIVITY∞

Creativity enlivens and awakens your soul. Allowing yourself time to be creative helps you to connect with your inner being and inspires you on the journey. Being creative connects you with a purity that over time we tend to lose as we become consumed with others' ideals and life in general. Creativity is needed to maintain inner peace and to reunite with the part of us still very much asleep. A creative activity helps you to reconnect with this lost facet, which in turn allows you to approach life differently and follow your bliss. It opens you up. What is great about creativity is you can completely let go and become lost in time. The activity can be anything you would like; music, painting, drawing, writing, decorating, the list is endless. Music and art in particular are prodigious ways to touch the etheric because music is able to mimic energy and frequencies that awaken the soul, while art can be a reflection of the vision of the Universe. Even listening to music or viewing art is enough to connect you with a deeper piece of yourself where greater knowledge and clarity from the Universe may reach and inspire you. Sometimes it is worth trying something new that perhaps you have always wanted to try but for whatever reason have not. You are never too old to try something new. I recently discovered a knack for painting even though as a child, I was no Picasso. As a result, I never thought I could or should paint. By allowing myself the freedom to try something in a different way, I uncovered a new gift. We are all creative in our own way, if we provide ourselves the time and opportunity, discoveries will be made.

Creativity can also help you in the process of letting go. It engages the spirit to explore every space that our overstimulated minds tend to escape. A creative activity removes the distractions around you, allowing you to access a different space that is typically out of reach when we are consumed by the rush of everyday life.

Create an environment or space that you connect with and feel at peace in. A place where you can focus on the spiritual and where the creative juices flow. It could be an entire room, or even just a corner or nook, but having a designated spiritual place is important. Whenever you enter this space, you then set the intention of peace and connection, which allows you to easily receive guidance and feel peace. Often, having a physical space that mirrors the etheric helps you to connect because in a sense, it makes the intangible, tangible. In my personal space, I am surrounded by crystals and meaningful objects that have a powerful, positive vibe that I have carefully chosen over time.

This space helps me to feel calm, protected, and at peace. When your outer environment conjures up these emotions, your inner being will respond accordingly. If creating a spiritual space is not for you, even if it is, there is something in each day that you can either use or transform into something profound. Creativity starts with inspiration and inspiration is all around you. A dragonfly flying past you, an overheard conversation containing a message you needed to hear, anything really. Just something special in each day, meant for you, to inspire you. It is up to you how these inspirational moments translate into creativity. The possibilities are endless.

Beauty

In understated simplicity,

It encompasses us all.

Even though at times, we forget to

Stop and be in awe.

It is there to remind us of the

Spark of Divinity

Housed in everyone and everything

Ever so beautifully.

∞BEAUTY∞

Beauty. Why does it matter? What makes it so important? Beauty is the Universe. Whenever you come across beauty, you are greeting a piece of the invisible force that infuses us all. Not only does encountering something beautiful bring greater joy to our day, but beauty holds valuable lessons for us as well. One of these lessons is the most beautiful places in the world simply **are**. They do not worry about appearances or try to change in order to fit in. They are as they were intended to be, an ocean, a mountain, a forest, or the desert. I know this sounds silly, but it is true, nonetheless. We need to be more like this. Simply being ourselves as we were intended to be, a Divine spark. In doing so, we become a beautiful beacon of light shining for others. Next is that **everything** contains something beautiful. You may not see it straight away, but if you look hard enough, there is always beauty present. Be open to seeing it. One of the best ways to find beauty is to explore the world. Whether you venture to a distant country or take a walk in a park, beauty is to be found everywhere.

Since beauty is everywhere, seek it. One of the best ways to see beauty is in nature. We would all benefit from spending more time in nature with all of its power and simplicity. Nature is God personified, so nature can be a very spiritual experience if we so choose. What makes the Universe and nature, in more physical terms, so beautiful? It is all energy. Energy creates the physical world we experience. Energy is found in nature, and energy contributes to all of the beauty surrounding us. Take all of the patterns present in nature; symmetry, spirals, numbers, all so perfect and beautiful, you cannot help but be mesmerized. There is power and simplicity in this beauty as it represents the magnitude of our Universe and the building blocks that form the foundation of our experience.

You see why we need greater beauty in our lives. There is so much darkness and negativity weighing the world down, and day to day people feed this negativity. The news is mostly negative, focusing on stories that do not uplift, but rather lower us. Hatred and violence are all too present. But, if we wish to ascend and awaken into a new, more enlightened state, then we must feed the light and welcome positivity into our lives and extend this to the world as a whole. Choose beauty and positivity. Not only can it be found in our natural surroundings, but it can also be found in the unlikeliest of places. Through attitude, kindness, and even the creative spark within. When we focus on beauty, life becomes more beautiful. We see that life is full of opportunities to experience beauty or bring about beauty. Even when you seem to be surrounded by negativity and unpleasantness, you can create the beauty the situation needs. Infuse it with positivity and light. Shine. Not only will you feel better, but others will feed off of your light and reflect it themselves. Imagine if everyone did this, how the world would respond. Our lives would change to mirror this new energy. <u>That</u> is beautiful.

A Life Lived

Life is meant to be lived

Fully in the moment.

No waiting and wondering,

Weighing all possibilities

Or life will pass you by.

You must forge your path,

Do what feels right.

So long as you live fully

In each moment,

You are living life right.

∞LIFE∞

Live. Do not waste your precious time on earth living someone else's truth. You can only fulfill your purpose in this cycle of life. Do what makes <u>you</u> happy. We have so little time, wasting it by carrying out activities or jobs that bring you no joy, but that also lack meaning, takes a piece of your light away. You will shine brighter and become whole once you choose to be happy and find an activity or job that is in line with your life's purpose. Do not be afraid to try new activities or roles. Sometimes when you do not know what you would like to do you have to branch out and try something different that you have never tried before. This new venture could bring you tremendous joy and lead you to your life's purpose and life of your dreams.

Life is meant to be enjoyed. Part of why children are so pure and happy is because they spend a great deal of time playing. This does not have to stop as we get older; we can still set aside time to be free and have fun. To be free and have fun also requires you live in the moment. If we are always looking ahead, or fixated on what is behind, we miss out on the opportunities in front of us now. The past is behind us, the future is unknown; the present moment is where life is; it is what we have now. Life is much more enjoyable when you are fully present in the here and now, as children are, because you are able to fully appreciate all you have in life instead of focusing on variables that cannot be changed. You become grateful for what you have now which in turn allows you to experience greater happiness.

Life should be full. Do not wait to find your bliss and follow your path. You do not know how life's events will play out, nor how much time you have, so live fully now. You never experience the exact same thing twice, so good or bad, the moment will eventually pass. In the bad moments, know that incredible experiences and moments lie before you, and your present situation is temporary. Be present, learn what you need to from it, and maintain a positive outlook. During the good moments, realize how blessed you are to be experiencing them because life will change at some point. We all must experience the highs and lows, so even the good moments must temporarily come to end. Know that they are meant to be enjoyed, with you engaged in each moment. When it is time for a challenge, and a good moment to be completed, know great moments are once again around the corner. A full life requires all forms of experiences and moments. Jump in. Learn. Enjoy. A lifetime of lessons and experiences are waiting for you.

Challenge your comfort zone. Some of life's greatest experiences lie just beyond our boundaries. Getting outside of your comfort zone to experience the world around you, even just to gain a different perspective, can lead you to a new level. Your eyes are opened to a broader world that brings about greater clarity because you are not confined within your limits. Make an effort to surprise yourself sometimes by taking that extra step. It could lead you somewhere incredible. At the very least, you will enjoy a fresh perspective that encompasses a more comprehensive view of life. Perhaps an epiphany or truth awaits.

Find a place where your soul is happy and at peace. Many people do not realize that while our soul's true home lies beyond this realm, there are places on earth that come close, and there is a place in the world for us all. When you find yours, your soul will come alive. This place will feel magnetic, like it is drawing you in. You will be energized and uplifted as your soul connects to it. Do not be afraid to travel the world to find it as the feeling and connection is worth searching for. When you find your place here on earth you will find it easier to connect with the spiritual and etheric, infusing your awakening with greater clarity and depth. Although you may not live in this place permanently, it will always be there as a retreat for you when you need to recharge.

Raise the vibration. You help to steer your life by the energy you bring. By raising your vibration to be positive and vivacious, you not only will attract more of this energy into your life, but you will also have an effect on the overall energy of the planet. As more people raise their own vibrations, the collective vibration will be raised as well, which means a more positive, love and light filled experience for us all. You can raise your vibration by engaging in activities that feed your soul. When your soul is happy, you are happy, and your energy is positive. Also, helping others and making the world a better place raises your vibration. In other words, do not just spread the light, be the light everyday.

∞EPILOGUE∞

Infinity

Our journey on earth will come to an end

But only so we may rise, recharge, and begin again.

Collect the lessons we learned along the way,

So our souls may awaken and advance

Growing closer to the Divine in every way.

When the physical journey comes to an end,

We will begin the trek into infinity

Which is both the beginning as well as

The end. ∞

∞EPILOGUE∞

The journey is infinite, even if finite on earth. Since time is a facade, it really is eternal. Our souls continue to learn and grow forever. We will build upon what we have learned, we will advance, the journey will continue. The pinnacle of the journey, whether earthbound or not is when we awaken to the entire realm that surrounds us and is within us. For it is only when we awaken and acknowledge the light within that we truly come alive. When this occurs, we see in a way different than before, we understand it is our oneness that unites us, and the individual journey is one piece that adds to the collective journey we are all experiencing together. Our journeys and missions as infinite beings dictate that we ascend as we awaken. This is our purpose. To awaken into the beings we have the potential to be. Through our journeys on earth, we collect lessons, undertake experiences, learn from our mistakes, and help one another to see our Divine nature. It is within us all, and through our earthly lives, we come closer to understanding this. Earth is but one facet of the journey, as our souls will continue to embody the lessons and experiences we collect while here, simply on another plane. When all is said and done, nothing material will matter. Our souls are the elements of us that travel into infinity. Our physical bodies and all that accompanies them will eventually cease to exist. They are vessels for us to use in order to awaken and to advance, so our souls may blossom. At some point, we are all called back "Home." This signals the end of our journey on earth. We return to where we all originated from, the Divine force that created us all. It is no different than on earth when we yearn to be home, it is where we feel at peace, where we re-charge, and where we make memories. On earth, we go through times where we just want to be at home, here on the physical plane. The same holds true for our other home, our etheric home. Our souls want to return Home, it is encoded in our being. We must return for a time to re-charge, cleanse, and receive a clean slate. After our journeys on earth, with all of the highs and lows, we need this step to shed this energy so we may begin again, energized and ready to continue our growth. From this place that incubates us after our adventure on earth is also the place that sends us back to earth where we will once again use the human experience to obtain greater wisdom and understanding so our souls may advance. It is for this reason that the intangible will be palpable and infinite as this infinite luminosity envelopes us all. This realm, this force, this mystery is both the beginning as well as the end...

∞NOTE FROM THE AUTHOR∞

Thank you for joining me on this journey. I hope you have experienced your personal awakening. Together may we all foster the people, cultivate the light, and change the world.

-Taylor Rose

If you are interested in learning more, or if you would like to schedule an appointment with Taylor, please visit www.infiniteluminos.com

CPSIA information can be obtained at www.ICGtesting.com
Printed in the USA
LVOW11*1935240316

480646LV00001B/1/P